my **revisi⏻n** notes

## AQA AS/A-level History

# FRANCE IN REVOLUTION

1774–1815

Dave Martin

Series editor:
David Ferriby

**HODDER**
EDUCATION
AN HACHETTE UK COMPANY

Every effort has been made to trace all copyright holders, but if any have been inadvertently overlooked, the Publishers will be pleased to make the necessary arrangements at the first opportunity.

Although every effort has been made to ensure that website addresses are correct at time of going to press, Hodder Education cannot be held responsible for the content of any website mentioned in this book. It is sometimes possible to find a relocated web page by typing in the address of the home page for a website in the URL window of your browser.

Hachette UK's policy is to use papers that are natural, renewable and recyclable products and made from wood grown in sustainable forests. The logging and manufacturing processes are expected to conform to the environmental regulations of the country of origin.

Orders: please contact Bookpoint Ltd, 130 Milton Park, Abingdon, Oxon OX14 4SE. Telephone: +44 (0)1235 827720. Fax: +44 (0)1235 400454. Email education@ bookpoint.co.uk Lines are open from 9 a.m. to 5 p.m., Monday to Saturday, with a 24-hour message answering service. You can also order through our website: www. hoddereducation.co.uk

ISBN: 978 1 4718 7625 7

© Dave Martin 2017

First published in 2017 by
Hodder Education,
An Hachette UK Company
Carmelite House
50 Victoria Embankment
London EC4Y 0DZ
www.hoddereducation.co.uk

Impression number  10 9 8 7 6 5 4 3 2 1

Year      2020 2019 2018 2017

Cover photo © Oleksii Sergieiev / Alamy Stock Photo
Illustrations by Integra
Typeset by Integra Software Services Pvt. Ltd., Pondicherry, India
Printed in India

A catalogue record for this title is available from the British Library.

# My revision planner

# Introduction

## Component 2: depth study

Component 2 involves the study of a significant period of historical change and development (around 20–25 years at AS and 40–50 years at A-level) and an evaluation of primary sources.

## France in Revolution, 1774–1815

The specification lists the content of this component in two parts, each part being divided into three sections.

### Part 1 The end of Absolutism and the French Revolution, 1774–95

1 The origins of the French Revolution, 1774–89
2 The experiment in constitutional monarchy, 1789–92
3 The emergence and spread of the Terror, September 1792–95

### Part 2 The rise of Napoleon and his impact on France and Europe, 1795–1815

4 The Directory and Napoleon's rise to power, 1795–99
5 The impact of Napoleon's rule on France, 1799–1815
6 The impact of Napoleon's rule on Europe, 1799–1815

Although each period of study is set out in chronological sections in the specification, an exam question may arise from one or more of these sections.

### The AS examination

The AS examination which you may be taking includes all the content in Part 1.

You are required to answer:
- Section A: one question on two primary sources: which is the more valuable? You need to identify the arguments in each source as well, as evaluating the provenance and tone. Using your knowledge in relation to these strands, you need to assess how valuable each source is, and then reach a judgement on which is the more valuable. The question is worth 25 marks.
- Section B: one essay question out of two. The questions will be set on a topic reflecting that this is a depth paper, and will require you to analyse whether you agree or disagree with a statement. Almost certainly, you will be doing both and reaching a balanced conclusion. The question is worth 25 marks.

The exam lasts one and a half hours, and you should spend about equal time on each section.

At AS, Component 2 will be worth a total of 50 marks and 50% of the AS examination.

### The A-level examination

The A-level examination at the end of the course includes all the content of both parts.

You are required to answer:
- Section A: one question on three primary sources: how valuable is each source? You are NOT required to reach a conclusion about which might be the most valuable. You need to identify the arguments in each source, as well as evaluating the provenance and tone. Using your knowledge in relation to these strands, you need to assess how valuable each source is. This question is worth 30 marks.
- Section B: two essay questions out of three. The questions will be set on a topic reflecting the fact that this is depth paper. The question styles will vary but they will all require you to analyse factors and reach a conclusion. The focus may be on causation, or consequence, or continuity and change.

The exam lasts for two and a half hours. You should spend about one hour on Section A and about 45 minutes on each of the two essays.

At A-level, Component 2 will be worth a total of 80 marks and 40% of the A-level examination.

In both the AS and A-level examinations you are being tested on the ability to:
- use relevant historical information (Sections A and B)
- evaluate different historical sources (Section A)
- analyse factors and reach a judgement (Section B).

## How to use this book

This book has been designed to help you develop the knowledge and skills necessary to succeed in the examination.
- The book is divided into six sections – one for each section of the A-level specification.
- Each section is made up of a series of topics organised into double-page spreads.
- On the left-hand page you will find a summary of the key content you will need to learn.
- Words in bold in the key content are defined in the glossary (see pages 106–108)
- On the right-hand page you will find exam-focused activities.

Together these two strands of the book will provide you with the knowledge and skills essential for examination success.

**▼ Key historical content**

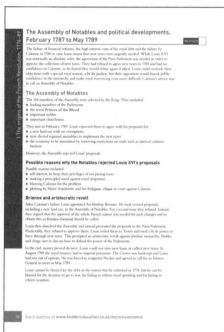

**▼ Exam-focused activities**

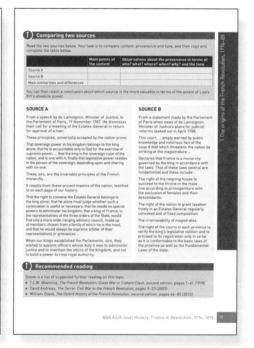

## Examination activities

There are three levels of exam focused activities:
- Band 1 activities are designed to develop the foundation skills needed to pass the exam. These have a green heading and this symbol.
- Band 2 activities are designed to build on the skills developed in Band 1 activities and to help you to achieve a C grade. These have an orange heading and this symbol.
- Band 3 activities are designed to enable you to access the highest grades. These have a purple heading and this symbol.

Some of the activities have answers or suggested answers starting on page 110. These have the following symbol to indicate this.

Each section ends with an exam-style question and sample answers with commentary. This will give you guidance on what is expected to achieve the top grade.

You can also keep track of your revision by ticking off each topic heading in the book, or by ticking the checklist on the contents page. Tick each box when you have:
- revised and understood a topic
- completed the activities.

Quick quizzes at **www.hoddereducation.co.uk/myrevisionnotes**

# Mark schemes

For some of the activities in the book it will be useful to refer to the mark schemes for this paper. Below are abbreviated forms.

## Section A Primary sources

| Level | AS level exam | A-level exam |
| --- | --- | --- |
| 1 | Describing source content or stock phrases about value of source; limited understanding of context. (1–5) | Some comment on value of at least one source but limited response; limited understanding of context. (1–6) |
| 2 | Some relevant comments on value of one source, or some general comments on both. Some understanding of context. (6–10) | Some relevant comments on value or one or two sources, or focus only on content or provenance, or consider all three sources in a more general way. Some understanding of context. (7–12) |
| 3 | Some relevant comments on value of sources, and some explicit reference to focus of question, with some understanding of context. Judgements thinly supported. (11–15) | Some understanding of all three sources in relation to content and provenance with some awareness of historical context. An attempt to consider value, but probably some imbalance across the three sources. (13–18) |
| 4 | Range of relevant, well-supported comments on value of sources for issue identified in question. Not all comments will be well-substantiated, and will have limited judgements. (16–20) | Good understanding of three sources in relation to content and provenance with awareness of historical context to provide a balanced argument on their value in relation to focus of question. One or more judgements may be limited in substantiation. (19–24) |
| 5 | Very good understanding of value of sources in relation to focus of question and contextual knowledge. Thorough evaluation, well-supported conclusion. (21–25) | Very good understanding of all three sources in relation to content and provenance and combines this with strong awareness of historical context to present balanced argument on their value in relation to focus of question. (25–30) |

## Section B Essays

| Level | AS-level exam | A-level exam |
| --- | --- | --- |
| 1 | Extremely limited or irrelevant information. Unsupported, vague or generalist comments. (1–5) | Extremely limited or irrelevant information. Unsupported, vague or generalist comments. (1–5) |
| 2 | Descriptive or partial, failing to grasp full demands of question. Limited in scope. (6–10) | Descriptive or partial, failing to grasp full demands of question. Limited in scope. (6–10) |
| 3 | Some understanding and answer is adequately organised. Information showing understanding of some key features. (11–15) | Understanding of question and a range of largely accurate information showing awareness of key issues and features, but lacking in precise detail. Some balance established. (11–15) |
| 4 | Understanding shown with range of largely accurate information showing awareness of some of key issues and features, leading to a limited judgement. (16–20) | Good understanding of question. Well-organised and effectively communicated, with range of clear and specific supporting information showing good understanding of key features and issues, with some conceptual awareness. (16–20) |
| 5 | Good understanding. Well-organised and effectively communicated. Range of clear information showing good understanding and some conceptual awareness. Analytical in style, leading to a substantiated judgement. (21–25) | Very good understanding of full demands of question. Well-organised and effectively delivered, with well-selected, precise supporting information. Fully analytical, with balanced argument and well-substantiated judgement. (21–25) |

# 1 The origins of the French Revolution, 1774–89

## Absolutism and the structure of the Ancien Régime, part 1

### The Ancien Régime

The Ancien Régime is the name used for the French system of government before the Revolution. It was first used in 1790, after the Revolution began, as an insult and means 'old rule' or 'old Régime'.

### Absolutism

The head of the Ancien Régime was the king, Louis XVI. In theory he was 'an **absolute monarch**'. At his coronation Louis swore an oath to God, not to his subjects. Absolutism means that there were no legal limits to the king's power over his subjects. In reality, Louis' power was limited by four factors:

- He had been taught to take advice on important decisions.
- His advisers/ministers came from a pool of career administrators and courtiers.
- He was bound by the laws and customs of France.
- He needed the consent of the noble elite.

### Louis XVI (1774–92)

Louis was born in Versailles in 1754. He became **dauphin** following the early deaths of his older brother and father. He succeeded his grandfather in 1774. He was well educated, fluent in English and Italian, enjoyed hunting and the hobby of lock making. In 1770 he married **Marie Antoinette**, daughter of the Austrian Empress Maria Theresa. This was unpopular, as Austria was blamed for France's defeat in the **Seven Years' War** (1753–63). It was 1778 before they had a child and 1781 before they produced a male heir.

Historians differ on his character and abilities:

- '… lacking in will; honest and well-intentioned, he was far from being a great mind.' Georges Lefebvre (1939)
- '… devoted to his subjects, committed to reform, more the victim of circumstance than his own failings.' Paul Hanson (2009)
- '… took an intelligent, if fluctuating interest in matters of government.' Peter Jones (2010)

### Government

Government consisted of Louis, his advisers and ministers. They were based in the palace of Versailles, 12 miles south west of Paris. Ministers did not meet to make decisions collectively. Instead, Louis met each individually to discuss the work of their department. So Louis decided the overall direction of government policy. This created the problem of ministers and **court factions** working against each other, not co-operating.

A second problem of government was the wide variation in laws and customs across France. France had no single representative body which could pass laws covering the whole country. All royal legislation had to be **ratified** by one of the 13 regional **parlements**. France was a patchwork of different forms of administration, different legal systems, different taxes and different rules on who paid them. So there was no single solution to any problem.

### Intendants

Previous kings had attempted to create one system by splitting the country into 36 **généralités** or administrative areas, each under the control of a royal official, an **intendant**. The intendants were responsible for carrying out government policy but they were hindered by local law courts and parlements and seen as overly authoritarian.

**Identify relevant content**

Read Source A and the question below.

Go through the source and highlight the sections that are relevant for the focus of the question, and annotate in the margin the main points.

How valuable is this source for understanding how Louis XVI ruled?

## SOURCE A

An extract from a letter written by Marie Antoinette to her brother Joseph II of Austria reporting on a session of the Paris Parlement four days earlier, attended by the King on 19 November 1787.

On Monday the king went to the Parlement to register two edicts: the first for loans to be spread over a five-year period in order to repay loans with a fixed date for redemption. There was a majority of opinions in favour of registration, but the king presides over the Parlement as he presides over his council, i.e. without being bound by the majority opinion. Consequently, after everyone had given his opinion, the king, without counting votes, said: 'I order the registration.' The duc d'Orleans dared to protest and say that this form was illegal.

...

The king has exiled him to Villers-Cotterets and forbids him to see anyone but his family and household. Two councillors in the Parlement, M. Fréteau and the Abbé Sabattier, had spoken with lack of respect in the king's presence; they have been conveyed to two fortresses.

 **Identify the significance of provenance**

(a) Look at what is said about Source B:
● Who wrote it
● What type of source it is
● When it was written
● Where it was written
● And – crucially – why: what was the speaker's purpose?

(b) What does this suggest about its value as a source of evidence?

## SOURCE B

From the book *Travels in France During the Years 1787, 1788 and 1789* by the Englishman Arthur Young, first published in 1792. He travelled through France and wrote about its people and the conduct of public affairs. Initially critical of the condition of the peasants, he came to oppose the violence of the Revolution. Here he criticises the power of intendants.

The kingdom was parcelled into generalities, with an intendant at the head of each, into whose hands the whole power of the crown was delegated for everything except the military authority; but particularly for all affairs of finance. ... The rolls of the *taille, capitation, vingtiemes*, and other taxes, were distributed among districts, parishes, and individuals, at the pleasure of the intendant, who could exempt, change, add, or diminish at pleasure. Such an enormous power, constantly acting, and from which no man was free, must, in the nature of things, degenerate in many cases into absolute tyranny. It must be obvious that the friends, acquaintances, and dependents of the intendant, and the friends of these friends, to a long chain of dependence, might be favoured in taxation at the expense of their miserable neighbours; and that noblemen in favour at court, to whose protection the intendant himself would naturally look up, could find little difficulty in throwing much of the weight of their taxes on others, ...

# Absolutism and the structure of the Ancien Régime, part 2

## Social divisions

French society was divided into three estates.

### The First Estate – the Clergy

The clergy formed less than 0.5 per cent of the population but the Church owned roughly one-tenth of French land. It controlled almost all education, most hospitals and **poor relief**. It had powers of censorship and published the government's messages. In many towns the clergy dominated while in the countryside the parish priest (**curé**) was influential.

### The Second Estate – the nobility

There were roughly 120,000 nobles, less than 1 per cent of the population, but they owned between a quarter and a third of French land.

- **Noblesse de court** at Versailles were very wealthy, provided the king's advisers, ambassadors, intendants and ministers and had access to royal patronage.
- **Noblesse de robe** were nobles created by the monarchy selling legal and administrative offices with a hereditary title. In 1789 there were over 70,000 **venal offices**.
- Most other nobles lived on their country estates. Many were not wealthy. They were jealous of court nobles, protective of their own status and privileges, and dependent on their **feudal rights**.

### The Third Estate

The Third Estate made up were the rest of society and consisted of nearly 28 million people. At the top were the **bourgeoisie**, mostly in towns. They were growing in wealth and numbers. They owned most industrial and all commercial capital, about one-fifth of all private French wealth and roughly a quarter of French land. Their ambition was to become part of the nobility.

In the countryside were the peasants, over 80 per cent of the population. The majority farmed at **subsistence** level and worked as labourers on the land, in industries or as migrant workers in towns.

In the towns were the small property owners, skilled workers and unskilled labourers.

## Privileges and burdens

The clergy paid no taxes. Instead the Church made a voluntary annual grant of about 16 million **livres**, just 5 per cent of total Church income.

The nobility were exempt from the heaviest tax, the taille (land tax), and the corvées royales (labour service on the roads). They paid some newer taxes linked to income but were often able to avoid paying the full amount. They were exempt from military conscription although many volunteered to fight by buying **commissions**.

The peasantry, the poorest in society, carried the heaviest burden. To the lord of the manor (the **seigneur**) they paid rents and taxes on their grain harvest and some had to do labour service. To the state they performed labour service on the roads and paid the taille and the gabelle (salt tax). They could be conscripted or have soldiers **billeted** upon them. They paid the **tithe** to the Church. Their main concern was to stay alive and this was dependent on the price of bread.

## Strengths and weaknesses

In 1783 France was arguably the most powerful European country and had just defeated Britain. Although the structure of the Ancien Régime was inefficient and unfair, it worked. However, the king could not make radical changes so its key weaknesses, the problems of government and of taxation, could not be reformed and tensions in society grew.

**Complete the paragraph** a

Below are a sample exam question and a paragraph written in answer to the question.

The paragraph contains a point and specific examples, but lacks a concluding analytical link back to the question. Complete the paragraph adding this link back to the question in the space provided.

'Ancien Régime France was a deeply divided society.' Explain why you agree or disagree with this view.

> The French nobility or Second Estate numbered over 100,000 people. It was made up of three types of noble. The noblesse de court lived at Versailles, had access to royal patronage and served as Louis' ministers. The noblesse de robe had bought their offices and in return had a noble title. This was one way the middle classes could join the nobility. Most nobles belonged to a third group, nicknamed 'sparrow hawks'. These tended to be poorer and lived on their estates across France. They were keen to protect their feudal rights. Overall the three groups ...
>
> _____
>
> _____

**Identify the tone and emphasis of a source**

Study Source A below. Focus on the:
- language
- sentence structure
- emphasis of the source
- overall tone.

What does the tone and emphasis of the source suggest about its value in terms of the:
- reliability of the evidence?
- utility of the evidence for studying Ancien Régime government?

### SOURCE A

From the journal of the Marquis de Castries, Minister responsible for the navy June 1780 to August 1787. He reports a conversation he had with Queen Marie Antoinette on the subject of his successor, 27 June 1787.

I said that if there were any possibility of a lawyer (homme de robe) succeeding me then I should consider myself obliged to tell the king that his navy would be ruined; that we needed at the head of this department a man who knew how to command, who was used to it and who had the authority to make himself obeyed, and that Marquis de Bouillé seemed to me to deserve preference over those of his rank whom the king could consider.

# The ideas of the Enlightened philosophes

## The Enlightenment

The Enlightenment was an intellectual movement that spread across Europe (c1740–c1789). Writers and thinkers challenged a wide range of views that were accepted at the time, about religion, nature and absolute monarchy. They considered the nature of society and people's relationships with each other, exploring ideas of freedom, liberty and equality. The Enlightenment had a particularly strong influence in France.

## Extent of influence in France – the philosophes

The leading Enlightenment writers and thinkers in France were the philosophes. Many of them contributed to the most important work of the French Enlightenment – The Encyclopaedia – edited by Diderot and published in 1750–72. Its aim was 'to change the way people think'. Articles dealt with topics like 'reason' but also with agricultural techniques, printing and metalworking. Its scientific approach directly challenged ideas held by the Church and other institutions and caused huge controversy. Some in the Church wanted it suppressed.

The most influential philosophes were Montesquieu, Voltaire and **Rousseau**. They expressed a deep dislike of organised religion and discussed how social and political institutions might be changed for the good of the people. They questioned the institutions of the Ancien Régime but did not advocate revolution.

- Montesquieu criticised royal absolutism but argued that it was the role of the aristocracy to limit royal power, not the people.
- Voltaire criticised the Catholic Church and religious intolerance but believed religion was necessary to preserve public morals. He defended royal authority.
- Rousseau went furthest. He argued that a **despotic** monarch could be overthrown by their subjects and that sovereignty resided in the people rather than in the person of the king.

The ideas of the philosophes reached a wider audience through their stories and plays. Voltaire's popular novel, *Candide*, was banned for blasphemy and Voltaire was imprisoned in the Bastille.

## Salons

Enlightenment ideas were spread through the **salons**. An aristocratic hostess would invite a range of guests, nobles and bourgeoisie to discuss art, literature and politics. Sometimes political decisions were taken and deals made between the king's ministers in salons.

The new ideas were also discussed in the increasing number of cafés and **Masonic Lodges** and in the growing numbers of newspapers – whereas there were only three in 1700, there were over 80 by 1785.

## The impact of the American Revolution and War of Independence

America was another source of ideas challenging the Ancien Régime. Louis XVI had taken the fateful decision to enter the War of Independence in 1778. The American colonies had been in revolt against British rule for two years and many in France were sympathetic to the colonists' cause of freedom (liberty) and democracy. Some idealistic French aristocrats, notably the **Marquis de Lafayette**, had already crossed the Atlantic to enlist in the American forces. When they and the 8,000 troops who served in America came home after 1783, they brought with them renewed ideas of liberty and democracy, plus the example and experience of the overthrow of an existing political authority and the building of a new order in its place.

# ! Mind map

Complete the mind map with brief detail or explanation to help answer the following question:

How influential were Enlightenment ideas in the period 1774–89?

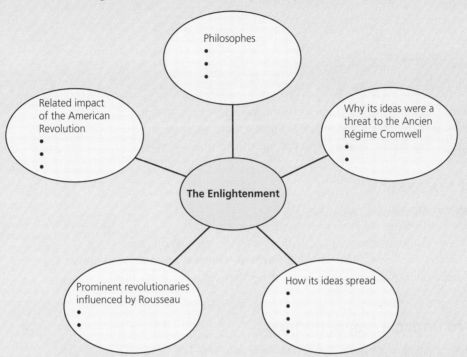

# i Moving from assertion to argument  a

Below are a sample exam question and a series of assertions made by the candidate, within a paragraph devoted to discussing Enlightenment ideas as part of their overall answer. Read the exam question and then add a justification to each of the assertions to turn it into an argument.

'Economic and financial problems were the most important factors that led to the start of the French Revolution.' Explain why you agree or disagree with this view.

The Enlightenment was an important factor in the coming of the French Revolution because ...

Among the Philosophes Rousseau believed that the people could overthrow a despotic ruler. This idea was dangerous because ...

People heard and read Enlightenment arguments in a variety of places such as ...

This was important because ...

In many ways the Enlightenment was an important/very important/crucial contributing factor to the coming of the Revolution.

# Economic problems and royal finance

## Royal debt

In 1774 Louis XVI's biggest problem was money. The monarchy was heavily in debt due to the costs of foreign wars.

| War | Estimated cost |
|---|---|
| War of Austrian Succession (1740–48) | 1 billion livres |
| Seven Years' War (1756–63) | 1.8 billion livres |

Louis could not pay off the debt. Even in peacetime royal income was not enough to cover expenditure, because of the size of the interest payments. In the short term the Crown borrowed from international banks, but in the long term this just made things worse.

## Inefficient tax system

Most royal income came from taxation. This was not enough because:
- the nobles, the king's richest subjects, were exempt from most taxes
- tax collection was chaotic and incomplete because of all the regional differences
- tax farming reduced the Crown's income. The **Farmers-General** paid an agreed sum in advance for the right to collect certain taxes. What they collected above that sum was their profit.

## Attempts to improve royal finances

Louis tried to follow a policy of reform to improve royal finances. The Controller General was the minister responsible.

### Turgot

In 1776 Louis appointed Anne-Robert-Jacques Turgot as Controller General. Turgot was influenced by the ideas of the **physiocrats**. He removed price controls, abolished guilds and proposed a new property tax. His reforms and the way he went about them aroused great hostility from those whose interests were threatened. Louis dismissed him.

### Necker

In 1776 **Jacques Necker**, a Swiss banker, was appointed. He tried a different route of reforming royal expenditure and increasing the royal share of farmed taxes. He tried to cut venal offices but this drew hostility from the nobles who held them.

Necker's key mistake was advising Louis that France could afford to enter the American War of Independence when it could not. This war cost an estimated 1.3 billion livres, so royal debt increased.

In 1781 Necker issued the first public report on royal finances to show that, in his view, they were in good order. However, some of the minor details of court expenditure were seized upon by enemies of the monarchy as examples of extravagant royal spending. This lost Necker the support of the court and he resigned.

### Calonne

From 1783 Louis' chief minister, the Vicomte de Calonne, managed the royal finances by selling offices and by lavish spending. The spending maintained confidence in the monarchy, which meant that it could raise loans. However, Calonne recognised that this could not continue indefinitely and that reform was still needed, hopefully when a number of taxes were due for renewal in 1787 – but events overtook him. Calonne was unsuccessful in raising loans in 1785 and early 1786. In August 1786 he told Louis that the government was close to bankruptcy.

## Support or challenge?

Below is a sample exam question which asks how far you agree with a specific statement. Below this are a series of general statements which are relevant to the question. Using your own knowledge and the information on the opposite page, decide whether these statements support or challenge the statement in the question.

How far do you agree that the decision in 1778 to enter the war against Britain was ultimately responsible for the failure of royal finances ten years later?

| | Support | Challenge |
|---|---|---|
| The war cost 1.3 billion livres | | |
| Louis XVI's ministers failed to make financial reforms | | |
| The French tax system was inefficient | | |
| Louis inherited a massive debt from his predecessors | | |
| The Parlement of Paris refused to agree to new taxes | | |

## Judgements on the value of a source

Read the source below and then the alternative answers that reflect the provenance of the source. Which answer will gain the highest level in the mark scheme, and why?

The source is valuable to a historian investigating the problems faced by Louis XVI in trying to reform taxation because it represents the view of the magistrates of Amiens. As such, it illustrates the rivalries between different groups, in this case the magistrates and the provincial assembly over local taxes.

The source is biased so it is not valuable to a historian.

The source is valuable to a historian investigating the problems faced by Louis XVI in trying to reform taxation. It's an official letter and gives the views of the magistrates of Amiens. It illustrates the rivalries between different groups and the complexity of Ancien Régime France, which made reform so difficult. It is less useful, however, for considering the opposition to tax reforms from the groups who were exempt, the clergy and the nobility.

### SOURCE A

From a letter sent by the municipal magistrates of Amiens to the king in 1787. In it, they are asserting their rights.

... a valuable right for our city, a right deriving from our constitution, a right founded on the most solemn formal laws, the right to be subject for our municipal Régime only to your direct authority and to the authority of the Council ... The provincial assembly ... pretends that our common lands and our taxes on goods entering the city form part of its jurisdiction.

# The Assembly of Notables and political developments, February 1787 to May 1789

REVISED

The failure of financial reforms, the high interest costs of the royal debt and the failure by Calonne in 1786 to raise loans meant that new taxes were urgently needed. While Louis XVI was notionally an absolute ruler, the agreement of the Paris Parlement was needed in order to approve the collection of new taxes. They had refused to agree new taxes in 1785 and had no confidence in Calonne, so he feared they would refuse again if asked. Louis could override their objections with a special royal session, a **lit de justice**, but their opposition would knock public confidence in the monarchy and make royal borrowing even more difficult. Calonne's advice was to call an Assembly of Notables.

## The Assembly of Notables

The 144 members of the Assembly were selected by the King. They included:

- leading members of the Parlements
- the seven **Princes of the Blood**
- important nobles
- important churchmen.

They met in February 1787. Louis expected them to agree with his proposals for:

- a new land tax with no exemptions
- new elected regional assemblies to implement the new taxes
- the economy to be stimulated by removing restrictions on trade such as internal customs barriers.

However, the Assembly rejected Louis' proposals.

## Possible reasons why the Notables rejected Louis XVI's proposals

Possible reasons included:

- self-interest, to keep their privileges of not paying taxes
- making a principled stand against royal despotism
- blaming Calonne for the problem
- plotting by Marie Antoinette and her **Polignac clique** at court against Calonne.

## Brienne and aristocratic revolt

After Calonne's failure Louis appointed Archbishop Brienne. He took revised proposals, including a new land tax, to the Assembly of Notables. For a second time they refused. Instead, they argued that the approval of the whole French nation was needed for such changes and to obtain this an **Estates-General** should be called.

Louis then dissolved the Assembly and instead presented the proposals to the Paris Parlement. Predictably, they refused to approve them. Louis exiled them to Troyes and used a lit de justice to force through new taxes. This prompted an aristocratic revolt against absolute monarchy. Nobles and clergy met to discuss how to defend the power of the Parlements.

In the end, money proved decisive. Louis could not raise new loans or collect new taxes. In August 1788 the royal treasury had to suspend payments. The Crown was bankrupt and Louis had run out of options. He was forced to reappoint Necker and agreed to call for an Estates-General to meet in May 1789.

Louis cannot be blamed for the debt or the system that he inherited in 1774, but he can be blamed for the decision to go to war, for failing to reform royal spending and for failing to reform taxation.

## Comparing two sources

Read the two sources below. Your task is to compare content, provenance and tone, and then copy and complete the table below.

|  | Main points of the content | Observations about the provenance in terms of who? what? where? when? why? and the tone |
|---|---|---|
| Source A |  |  |
| Source B |  |  |
| Main similarities and differences |  |  |

You can then reach a conclusion about which source is the more valuable in terms of the extent of Louis XVI's absolute power.

### SOURCE A

From a speech by de Lamoignon, Minister of Justice, to the Parlement of Paris, 19 November 1787. He dismisses their call for a meeting of the Estates-General in return for approval of a loan.

These principles, universally accepted by the nation prove:

That sovereign power in his kingdom belongs to the king alone; that he is accountable only to God for the exercise of supreme power; ... that the king is the sovereign ruler of the nation, and is one with it; finally that legislative power resides in the person of the sovereign, depending upon and sharing with no-one.

These, sirs, are the invariable principles of the French monarchy ...

It results from these ancient maxims of the nation, testified to on each page of our history:

That the right to convene the Estates General belongs to the king alone; that he alone must judge whether such a convocation is useful or necessary; that he needs no special powers to administer his kingdom; that a king of France, in the representatives of the three orders of the State, would find only a more wide-ranging advisory council, made up of members chosen from a family of which he is the head, and that he would always be supreme arbiter of their representations or grievances ...

When our kings established the Parlements, sirs, they wished to appoint officers whose duty it was to administer justice and to maintain the edicts of the kingdom, and not to build a power to rival royal authority.

### SOURCE B

From a statement made by the Parlement of Paris when news of de Lamoignon, Minister of Justice's plans for judicial reforms leaked out in April 1788.

This court, ... amply warned by public knowledge and notorious fact of the coup d'état which threatens the nation by striking at the magistrature ...

Declares that France is a monarchy governed by the king in accordance with the laws. That of these laws several are fundamental and these include:

The right of the reigning house to succeed to the throne in the male line according to primogeniture with the exclusion of females and their descendants.

The right of the nation to grant taxation freely in an Estates General regularly convoked and of fixed composition.

The irremovability of magistrates.

The right of the courts in each province to verify the king's legislative volition and to proceed to its registration only in so far as it is conformable to the basic laws of the province as well as the Fundamental Laws of the state.

## Recommended reading

Below is a list of suggested further reading on this topic.

- T.C.W. Blanning, *The French Revolution: Class War or Culture Clash*, second edition, pages 1–61 (1998)
- David Andress, *The Terror: Civil War in the French Revolution*, pages 9–23 (2005)
- William Doyle, *The Oxford History of the French Revolution*, second edition, pages 66–85 (2012)

# The state of France by the meeting of the Estates-General

## Politically

Once the decision to call the Estates-General had been taken, Louis XVI and Neckar waited. Meanwhile they made some important decisions.

- They agreed to allow the Third Estate to have twice as many deputies as either of the other two Estates.
- They left the question of whether the Estates should vote by order or by head to be decided at its first meeting, a crucial mistake. If they voted by order the first two estates could outvote the Third Estate. If they voted by head, as individual deputies, then the Third Estate equalled the numbers of the first two estates.
- They made no attempt to influence the elections.
- They failed to draw up proposals for the Estates-General to consider when it met.

## Socially

Alongside absolutism and an unfair tax system, the other major source of resentment in French society was corruption at court and in the Church. The system of selling offices (venality) provided income for the monarchy and a bloc of supporters, but also led to wasteful corruption and blocked the advancement of those with talent.

There were complaints about the Church. Curés complained they were poor because they did not receive the entire tithe. Instead, the archbishops, bishops and abbots who often collected it kept most. These higher clergy enjoyed huge incomes which made such positions very desirable. As they were in the personal gift of the king they were secured by court nobles as careers for their younger sons. This led to problems of **absenteeism** and pluralism.

The privileges of the court nobles were resented by other nobles. Meanwhile, the privileges of the nobility were resented by all the other classes, especially the peasants.

## Economically

Poor harvests between 1770 and 1789 were a major reason for increased rural poverty.

A longer-term issue was land holding. On a man's death his land was divided equally among his heirs rather than going to the eldest son. The cumulative effect of this was smaller estates. By 1789 roughly a quarter of French farmland was owned by small peasant farmers and much of the rest rented out in small plots. This led to subsistence farming with no incentive to make improvements in methods or crops. Agricultural problems also adversely affected the woollen industry which added to rural poverty.

### Towns

There was a dramatic growth of towns in the eighteenth century. Towns grew because of the growth in industries – for example, silk in Nîmes – and in foreign trade in ports like Nantes. This growth led to problems and tensions in urban populations.

Most of France's wealthiest and best educated people lived in towns – the nobles and bourgeoisie, a few manufacturers and the skilled craftsmen who were organised into guilds. Besides them there were small property owners, shop keepers and artisans. However, the majority of the populations of towns were unskilled workers and poor. They lived in over-crowded and unhealthy conditions. They depended heavily on bread and any sudden rises in prices would trigger public disorder.

### Conditions in 1789

The harvest of 1788 was disastrous. The weather in the early months of 1789 was the coldest in living memory and food prices steadily rose to a high point on 14 July 1789.

## Identify the tone and emphasis of a source

Study the source below. Don't focus on the content; instead focus on the:

- language
- sentence structure
- emphasis of the source
- overall tone.

What does the tone and emphasis of the source suggest about its value in terms of the:

- reliability of the evidence
- utility of the evidence for studying attitudes towards reform?

### SOURCE A

From Memorandum of the Princes of the Blood, sent to the King on 12 December 1788.

Sire, the State is in peril. Your person is respected, the virtues of the monarch assure him of the homage of the nation. But Sire, a revolution is being prepared in the principles of government; it is being accomplished through the turmoil in men's minds. Institutions which were considered sacred and which have enabled this monarchy to prosper for so many centuries, have been put into question or are even described as unjust.

The writings which appeared during the Assembly of Notables ... the demands put forward by various provinces, towns or corporations; the subject matter and style of these demands; everything proclaims, all prove that there is a deliberate plan of insubordination and contempt for the laws of the State. ...

 ## RAG – rate the timeline

Below are a sample exam question and a timeline. Read the question, study the timeline and, using three coloured pens, put a red, amber or green star next to the events to show:

- red: events and policies that have no relevance to the question
- amber: events and policies that have some significance to the question
- green: events and policies that are directly relevant to the question.

'It was the actions of the Paris Parlement that forced Louis XVI to agree to call an Estates-General.' Explain why you agree or disagree with this view.

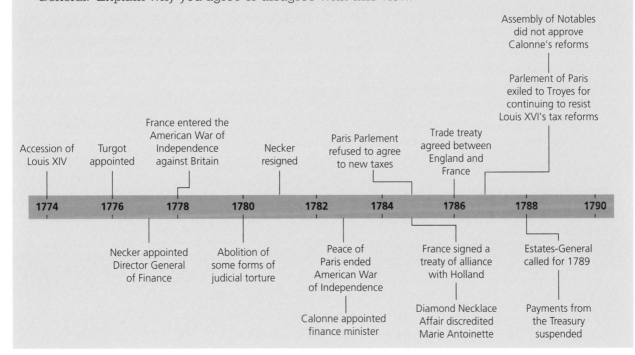

# Exam focus

Below is a sample Level 4 essay. It was written in response to an AS question.

'The ideas of the Enlightened philosophes seriously undermined the monarchy of Louis XVI.' Explain why you agree or disagree with this view.

The Enlightened philosophes were French writers and thinkers like Rousseau and Voltaire. They were part of a European movement of thinkers who were challenging a wide range of views that were accepted at the time about religion and nature and absolute monarchy. Many of them contributed to the Encyclopedia which the Church wanted suppressed.

The ideas of the philosophes were spread through France in a variety of ways. They wrote books as well as contributing to the Encyclopaedia and these books were read by the educated classes, the nobility and the bourgeoisie. Their ideas were also discussed in the salons where these people, including the king's ministers, met. They were also discussed in the Masonic Lodges. There was a real growth in the number of these in French cities and towns and the Duc D'Orleans was Grand Master of them. The last way in which their Enlightenment ideas were spread was in novels and plays, and Voltaire ended up imprisoned in the Bastille for the mockery of religion in his novel, *Candide*.

In their writings the philosophes showed a great dislike for organised religion, hence the Catholic Church's hostility to them. More importantly in discussing how political institutions could be changed for the good of the people, they directly challenged the institution of the absolute monarchy of Louis XVI. They were not arguing for a revolution, though – they saw it as the role of the nobility to limit royal power through the parlements rather than the ordinary people. Only Rousseau went further. He argued that a despotic monarch could be overthrown by their people and in his Social Contract wrote that sovereignty rested in the people, rather than the person of the king. He certainly influenced many people including future revolutionaries such as Robespierre and Madam Roland.

Some historians have argued that a book like the Social Contract was not widely read and have down played the influence of Enlightenment ideas but the same ideas were in the plays and novels that the philosophes wrote and these were very popular. For example, Rousseau's best-selling novel *Emile* advocated men and women being educated for citizenship, to take an active role in political affairs. This certainly worried the government. They feared its influence and his books were banned and publicly burned.

On the other hand, some argue that Louis XVI's monarchy was undermined by other factors. He inherited a number of problems, most importantly that the system of taxation was unfair, with the burden falling heaviest on those least able to carry it, the peasants. The first two estates, the clergy and the nobility, had the privilege of paying little or no tax and this was seen as unjust by many in French society. Louis and his ministers had tried to make some changes to the tax system, but the ministers were defeated by the vested interests ranged against them and, crucially, Louis failed to support them. Similarly, Louis' attempts at government reforms were hampered by the different legal and administrative systems in different parts of the country. So, new ideas such as those of the philosophes would gain more of a hearing if there was already widespread dissatisfaction with the current situation.

The essay jumps into a description of the philosophes. There is no real introduction, and certainly no suggestion of the argument to be developed beyond the hint in the last line.

This paragraph, and those that follow, would have been better started with a judgement on how significant this spreading of Enlightenment ideas was. Again, there are hints that influential people discussed them and that the government saw them as dangerous enough as to imprison a writer.

Precise detail would have strengthened this point – for example, 18 lodges in Versailles and 33 in Lyon in 1789.

This argument is really well made with specific evidence to support the idea that the philosophes challenged absolute monarchy.

Interesting detail although there is a danger of moving away from the central point.

The argument is well made in this paragraph, with explicit links made between the idea, its popularity and the government response.

This paragraph is showing that there is some balance to the essay, but this point could be better argued.

Louis himself undermined the prestige of the monarchy. He was physically unimposing and was seen as a figure of fun by some of his courtiers, for example, over the length of time it took him to consummate his marriage and produce an heir. He spent much of his time hunting and lock making and did not take the consistent interest in state affairs that they required. Nor did he back his ministers to force through the necessary changes, although perhaps that never was possible. The lavish expenditure of the court did not help.

It is true that the ideas of the Enlightened philosophes did undermine the monarchy of Louis XVI. At a time when France had a number of problems that the king and his government had failed to solve, these new ideas did gain an influence over people's thinking. However, they were not the only source of new ideas, as Frenchmen returning from the American War of Independence brought back with them ideas of liberty and democracy and experience of how an old order could be replaced with a new one. These, together with the failing of Louis himself, were also important.

> Some precise detail to support this valid point would strengthen the answer.

> The conclusion does reach some judgement, although it does not explicitly address the terms of the question. Moreover, it confuses the issue by introducing a new, albeit relevant, idea.

**The comments made during the essay could imply that the answer is weak. It is true that there are weaknesses:**

- The lack of a clear introduction.
- Some vagueness in explaining the significance of the Enlightenment ideas.
- Evidence is not always well linked to the question.
- Missed opportunities to provide links and precise final judgements.

**However, there are clear strengths:**

- There is a clear understanding overall on what the question is asking – whether the ideas undermined the monarchy or whether others factors were responsible.
- It deploys a range of accurate information.
- It is generally analytical in intention (even if not always successful in clear explanation).
- It is organised and mostly written in appropriate English.

### Moving from a Level 4 to Level 5

The exam focus essay at the end of Section 3 (page 56) provides a Level 5 essay. The essay here achieves a Level 4. Read both essays and the comments provided. Make a list of the additional features required to push a Level 4 essay into Level 5.

# Exam focus

Below is a sample Level 5 essay. It was written in response to an A-level question.

How important was the decision to go to war in 1778 in forcing Louis XVI to call an Estates-General?

The decision by Louis XVI and his ministers to go to war against Britain in 1778 was understandable, as it was an opportunity to get revenge on Britain for defeat in the Seven Years' War – and France did win. But the cost of the war was massive and this led to an increase in the royal debt, which was why Louis had to call the Estates-General. So it was a critical mistake but it was not the only one. Louis made a number of other mistakes and the actions of others also forced the calling of the Estates-General, notably the aristocratic revolt.

This starts with a good clear judgement from the outset. It also signals the direction that the essay is going to take.

In 1778 Louis had been on the throne for four years and he had already been trying to reform the royal finances, first with his minister Turgot and, when Turgot's reforms aroused so much hostility, Jacques Necker. The royal debt he inherited was huge, accumulated from the costs of earlier wars, and even in peacetime royal income did not meet expenditure. The war against Britain cost an estimated 1.3 billion livres, so this made the financial problem much worse as the royal debt grew. By 1788, when the Crown went bankrupt, interest payments on the debts accounted for more than half of royal income. It was bankruptcy that forced Louis to call the Estates-General, so it is possible to make a direct link between that and the declaration of war. However, it is important to remember that other things happened in the decade between them, too – other factors played a part.

Good use of specific evidence to support the view.

Explicit link made to the question and reiteration of line of argument that other factors were important, too.

Louis made a number of attempts to reform royal finances. The system of taxation was inefficient and unfair. Despite France being a rich country, royal income was not enough. There were three reasons for this. First, the Clergy and the nobility were exempt from most taxes and when Louis tried to make reforms, they resisted them. For example, Turgot wanted to introduce a property tax, which was understandably very unpopular with the nobility and clergy who owned the bulk of the land. They resisted these tax changes and Louis failed to support Turgot. You could argue that this was a mistake, but you might also say that Louis did need the support of the nobility to rule – that he was not an absolute monarch.

This offers an attempt at a balanced view of Louis XVI's decisions.

The second reason was that the system of tax collection was a mess. France was a collection of all sorts of administrative areas and different taxes were due in different places. This made collection and enforcement very difficult to achieve. The third and final reason is the system of tax farming. The Farmers-General paid an agreed sum of money to the Crown in return for the right to collect a tax. The difference between this and what they collected was their profit. Both of these reasons reduced how much tax income the Crown received.

An example would strengthen the answer here – for example, that Brittany was exempt from the salt tax, the gabelle, while its neighbouring regions were not and that this led to salt smuggling.

After Turgot's efforts to raise royal income the new minister, Necker, tried to reduce royal expenditure by cutting the number of venal offices. Venal offices were posts bought by people to become nobility. They were sold by the Crown in the first place and their holders were not likely to give them up without a fight. So, Necker's plans met with hostility from the nobility, too. This is important, as it was the later aristocratic revolt that forced Louis to call the Estates-General.

Introduces the counter-argument.

Quick quizzes at **www.hoddereducation.co.uk/myrevisionnotes**

Calonne followed Necker and he adopted a new strategy. He funded government by selling offices and by lavish spending. He did this to maintain confidence in the monarchy so that it could raise loans. He knew that this borrowing could not be sustained for ever, but was banking on the opportunity to reform taxation in 1787 when a number of taxes were due for renewal. However, events overtook his plans and in 1786 he told Louis that the Crown was on the brink of going bankrupt. As I've argued earlier, this bankruptcy was crucial. Without finance Louis could not maintain his government, so while the declaration of war was important, so too were the failures to reform taxation and finance.

Calonne and Louis knew the nobility in the Parlement of Paris were hostile to plans for taxation changes, including a land tax payable by all landowners without exemptions, so they came up with the solution of the Assembly of Notables – 144 carefully selected important nobles and clerics, including the king's brothers. Historians differ on why the Notables did not support Louis, but a number of factors were at work. Some were hostile to Calonne and thought him incompetent, some were probably putting their own selfish interests first, others were playing politics for their own advantage and some were making a genuine stand against royal despotism. For this last group, the ideas of the Enlightenment were clearly an influence. The philosophe Montesquieu had argued that it was the responsibility of the nobility to limit royal power. The result was that the Notables concluded that an Estates-General was required to consider important changes for France. Louis was very disappointed by this, changed his minister and tried to get new taxes approved by the Parlement of Paris. Predictably, they refused and Louis was left with no option. He could not raise loans, the Crown was bankrupt and the nobility were committed to defending the power of the Parlement. Historians call this the aristocratic revolt.

In conclusion, Louis' decision to go to war in 1778 was a major mistake because of the costs so it was a very important reason why he was forced to call the Estates-General. However, if he had been able to make the necessary reforms to royal finances through raising taxes, then he might have been able to avoid bankruptcy and resist the aristocratic revolt and the calls for reform for much longer.

> The answer avoids the danger of lapsing into narrative by bringing the focus back to the question.

> The conclusion is under developed but it is nevertheless a clear judgement.

This is an excellent piece of writing – consistently focused, well organised and written in a mature style. The premise of the question has been fully explored and challenged in an interesting manner. The response is well supported with precise factual details of events. It is consistently analytical and leads to a substantiated judgement that the decision was important. The conclusion could have been more developed, however. The answer clearly merits a Level 5.

### Sustaining an argument

The sign of a strong Level 5 answer is the way it sustains an argument from start to finish, with each paragraph developing a key part of the argument. Examine the opening and closing paragraphs carefully and highlight where the candidate has presented and concluded the argument. In addition, give a heading to each paragraph to indicate which part of the argument is being developed.

# 2 The experiment in constitutional monarchy, 1789–92

## The revolution, May–June 1789: developments in Versailles

### The opening of the Estates-General, 5 May 1789

At the time of the elections the three orders were asked to draw up a list of grievances and suggestions for reform, the **cahiers**.

- The First Estate was dominated by parish priests. They wanted higher stipends, access to the higher offices of the Church, greater Church control of education and a limit to the toleration of Protestantism.
- The Second Estate was dominated by deputies from long-standing noble families who held conservative views. About a third were liberals who were willing to give up their financial privileges. They were divided over Third Estate demands for tax reforms and a modern constitution.
- The Third Estate deputies were lawyers, landowners and office holders plus a few nobles and clergy. The electoral system excluded workers and peasants.

All three estates wanted a king whose powers were limited by an elected assembly which had the power to raise taxes and pass laws.

When they met at Versailles, Louis failed to put forward a programme of action for discussion. There was no mention of a new constitution, just unspecified talk of fairer taxation. The deputies of the Third Estate seized the initiative.

### The National Assembly, 17 June 1789

The three estates were meant to meet separately, but the Third Estate argued that all deputies needed to have their **election credentials** verified in a common session, with all three estates together. This would set a precedent for future discussions and create the likelihood of voting by head rather than by order. The nobility voted 188 to 46 against this. So did the clergy, 133 votes to 114. Meanwhile, the Third Estate refused to do anything until the other orders joined them. For a month there was deadlock. Louis was inactive.

On 10 June the Third Estate voted to begin verifying deputies' credentials without the clergy and nobles. A few clergy joined them. On 17 June the Third Estate voted 490 to 90 to call themselves the National Assembly. They claimed to represent the French nation and to have the right to decide taxation, a direct challenge to the king. Two days later the clergy voted to join them.

### The Tennis Court Oath

Louis tried to regain the initiative by holding a **séance royale**. Preparations involved closing, without explanation, the meeting room of the Third Estate (now the National Assembly). Angry at what they saw as a despotic act, the deputies moved to a nearby tennis court and swore an Oath not to disperse until they had given France a constitution.

In the royal session that followed, Louis offered concessions on taxes but said that the decrees of the National Assembly on 17 June were unacceptable and therefore void. Then the deputies were ordered to return to their separate rooms. They refused. More clergy and nobles joined the Third Estate, until by 27 June it numbered 830. Then Louis ordered the remaining clergy and noble deputies to join them.

## ! Delete as applicable **a**

Read the sample exam question and answer. Decide which of the possible options [in bold] is most appropriate. Delete the inappropriate options and finish the paragraph justifying your choices.

How successful were the deputies of the Third Estate in taking the initiative in 1789?

The deputies of the Third Estate were successful to a **great/fair/limited** extent. For example it was they who argued that all the deputies should have their election returns validated in a common session and they who refused to do anything when the other two orders voted against this idea. They also took the initiative to start validating deputies credentials without the other two orders. Other deputies from the clergy began to join them and some nobles too so Louis ended up ordering all three orders to meet as one. They also asserted their right, in the Tennis Court oath, to control taxation. In this way the deputies of the Third Estate were **extremely/moderately/slightly** successful because…

## ⸸ Judgements on the value of a source **a**

Read Source A below, the question and then the alternative answers that reflect on the provenance of the source. Which answer will gain the higher mark scheme level and why?

How valuable is this source to the historian trying to find out what people were complaining about in France in 1789?

The source is valuable to a historian investigating what people were complaining about in France. These are the views of one village who are concerned about taxation and privileges. The cahier was written to be presented at the Estates-General so it will be an accurate record.

The source is partially valuable to a historian trying to find out what people were complaining about in France in 1789 because it reflects the views of one parish. It shows the concerns many people had about the Ancien Régime, that taxes were not paid by everyone. It also supports the hostility to feudal rights as keeping a dovecote was one that many peasants resented, as the birds ate their seed. However, this is just one village close to Paris so it may not be typical.

### SOURCE A

From the cahier of the parish of Vitry-sur-Seine. The cahiers were books of grievances drawn up by each parish as part of the electoral process for the Estates General in 1789. Items 4, 7 and 9 are from a longer list.

4. The total suppression of all privileges whatsoever. Our parish contains fifty bourgeois properties with the best land of the locality without paying taxes.

Another sort of privilege are the exemptions from parish dues, which we expressly ask to be abolished. It is the well-to-do inhabitants of the parish who, to get out of paying these dues, buy an office in the town militia, or the mint, or in the administration of the gabelle, the aides, etc.

7. Total destruction of all rabbits.

9. Total abolition of … the right to keep a dovecote.

# The revolution, July 1789: developments in Versailles and Paris

## Revolt in Paris – the storming of the Bastille, 14 July 1789

Louis took action in the last week of June moving more troops into the Paris/Versailles area. It was clear that he was planning to dissolve the National Assembly, using force if necessary.

### 11 July

With over 20,000 troops in the area, Louis felt strong enough to dismiss the popular minister, Necker. Louis did not want to implement his reforms.

### 12 July

News of Necker's dismissal reached Paris and inflamed a tense situation. High food prices had already led to rioting. Necker was seen as the minister to solve the economic crisis.

Armed revolt was triggered by the oratory of Camille Desmoulins. He claimed that a massacre of the supporters of reform was planned. People armed themselves, there were violent clashes with royal troops and the hated **customs posts** around the city were attacked. When the **Gardes-françaises** were ordered to withdraw from Paris, many disobeyed and joined the people. That evening the Paris electors set up a **citizen's militia** to maintain order.

### 13 July

Barricades were erected to stop any more royal troops entering Paris. In Versailles the National Assembly called for the removal of all troops.

### 14 July

Parisians seized muskets and cannon from the arsenal, Les Invalides, then went to the Bastille for the gunpowder and cartridges stored there. It was a royal fortress and prison, a symbol of royal power. As the crowds massed around it, other royal troops in the city were withdrawn south of the River Seine. Their officers could not rely on their men to fire on the crowds. The Bastille governor refused to hand over any gunpowder, but when a group got into an inner courtyard he panicked and ordered his men to open fire. In total, 93 were killed. The people, supported by the Gardes-françaises, used cannon fire to storm the prison. De Launay, the Governor, surrendered and was murdered. The stormers of the Bastille were the **sans-culottes**. Roughly 250,000 Parisians had joined in this first **journée** of the Revolution. Louis had lost control of the city.

### 15 July

Louis visited the National Assembly to announce he was withdrawing all troops from Paris and Versailles. In Paris the electors formed themselves into the new revolutionary council, the **Commune**, and turned the citizen's militia into the National Guard, commanded by Lafayette. They wanted to keep the sans-culottes under control.

### 17 July

Louis now had to share power with the National Assembly. He recalled Necker and visited Paris, where he recognised the legality of the Commune and the National Guard. One observer, Gouverneur Morris, wrote, 'You may consider the Revolution to be over, since the authority of the King and the nobles has been utterly destroyed.' The Comte d'Artois, Louis's youngest brother, went into exile, as did many other nobles in the following weeks. They believed the royal cause was lost.

## Simple essay style

Below is a sample exam question. Use your own knowledge and the information on the opposite page to produce a plan for this question. Choose four general points and provide three pieces of specific information to support each general point.

Once you have planned your essay, write the introduction and conclusion for the essay. The introduction should list the points to be discussed in the essay. The conclusion should summarise the key points and justify which point was the most important.

> How accurate is it to say that, with the fall of the Bastille, the revolution was over and the power of the monarchy overthrown?

## Identify the significance of provenance

(a) Look at what is said about Source A:
● Who said it?
● What type of source is it?
● When was it said?
● Where was it said?
● And – crucially – why? What was the speaker's purpose?

(b) What does this suggest about its value as a source of evidence?

### SOURCE A

From the first edition of one of the many new newspapers, *Les Révolutions de Paris*, that sprang up in Paris in July 1789. The young journalist from Bordeaux, Elysée Loustallot, describes the aftermath of the storming of the Bastille.

On arriving, these people who were so impatient to avenge themselves allowed neither de Launay nor the other officers to go into the city court; they tore them from the hands of their conquerors and trampled them underfoot one after the other; de Launay was pierced by countless blows, his head was cut off and carried on the end of a spear, and his blood ran everywhere. And there were already two bodies being shown there before the disarmed guards from the Bastille appeared. They arrived, and the people demanded their execution, but the generous French Guards asked for their pardon, and on their request votes were taken, and the pardon was unanimous.

This glorious day must surprise our enemies, and portends finally the triumph of justice and freedom.

This evening, the city will be illuminated.

# The revolution, July–October 1789: developments in the country

## Developments in the country

Across France, towns and cities copied Paris and set up revolutionary committees and a National Guard to maintain order and to prevent counter-revolution by royalists. The king's intendants abandoned their posts as royal authority collapsed.

## The Great Fear

In the countryside there was violent unrest in response to high food prices, due to the bad harvest of 1788. The calling of the Estates-General raised hopes and kept violence in check until July. Then news of the king's surrender and the defeat of the nobility triggered the Great Fear. Rumours spread that gangs of **brigands** had been hired by fleeing nobles to take revenge by destroying the harvest. Peasants armed themselves and attacked the hated symbols of feudal power. Chateaux and documents recording feudal obligations were burned but few people, nobles or their agents, were killed.

## The abolition of feudalism

News of the violence reached the National Assembly deputies. They wanted to crush the rural revolt but didn't want to use royal troops in case those troops were used against them. They decided to gain the support of the peasants by giving them what they wanted – the abolition of **feudalism**.

On 4 August the National Assembly voted for the August Decrees.
- Feudal rights on people were abolished.
- Tithes, hunting rights, seigneurial courts, were abolished.
- All citizens were to be taxed equally.
- All were eligible for any office in the Church, state or army.

### The Declaration of the Rights of Man and the Citizen, 26 August 1789

The next task facing the deputies was to draft a new constitution. Their first step was the Declaration of the Rights of Man and the Citizen. All citizens were equal. These decrees formally dismantled the Ancien Régime.

## The October days

The deputies knew they needed the agreement of the king for their decrees. On 11 September they voted to allow Louis a suspensive **veto**. He could delay laws for up to four years, but could not veto them completely. They wanted a **constitutional monarchy**.

In Paris the National Guard struggled to maintain order, especially as bread shortages triggered riots. Meanwhile, journalists like Desmoulins and **Marat** reported on National Assembly debates and portrayed the supporters of a royal veto as unpatriotic. They advocated direct action by the people. In this atmosphere Louis summoned loyal troops to Versailles. Their protection gave him the confidence to refuse to accept some of the August Decrees and to question the Rights of Man declaration.

This triggered a violent reaction, a second Journée. Women in Paris seized weapons and marched on Versailles. The National Guard would not stop them. In Versailles the deputies of the National Assembly had to welcome them. Louis was forced to agree to the August Decrees. Next day the crowd broke into the palace and the Queen was threatened. The National Guard restored order, but both the royal family and the deputies were forced to go to Paris. They were now prisoners of the people of Paris.

**Identify the significance of provenance**

(a) Look at what is said about Source A:
- Who said it?
- What type of source is it?
- When was it said?
- Where was it said?
- And – crucially – why? What was the speaker's purpose?

(b) What does this suggest about its value as a source of evidence?

## SOURCE A

From a letter written by the steward of the Duke of Montmorency, 2 August 1789 to his master. Here he describes what the peasants have been doing.

Sir, so as not to disturb your peace, I have not revealed to you the justifiable concerns that have been perturbing me for some time, but now I would believe it unwise to leave you unaware. Brigandage and pillage are practised everywhere. The populace, attributing to the lords of the kingdom the high price of grain, is fiercely hostile to all that belongs to them. All reasoning fails: this unrestrained populace listens only to its own fury and, in all our province, the vassals are so outraged that they are prepared to commit the greatest excesses; moreover, in this very parish, persuaded that the Baron of Breteuil and his family are in the castle, it is said aloud that it will be set on fire. ...

Just as I was going to finish my letter, I learnt ... that approximately 300 brigands from all the lands associated with the vassals of the marquise de Longaunay have stolen the titles of rents and allowances of the *seigneurie,* and demolished her dovecotes ...

 **Spectrum of importance**    **a**

Below are a sample exam question and a list of general points which could be used to answer the question. Use your own knowledge and the information on the opposite page to reach a judgement about the importance of these general points to the question posed. Write numbers on the spectrum below to indicate their relative importance. Having done this, write a brief justification of your placement, explaining why some of these factors are more important than others. The resulting diagram could form the basis of an essay plan.

How influential in France were the ideas of the Enlightenment philosophes in the years 1788 and 1789?

1 The number of Masonic lodges, theatres and bookshops in towns and cities

2 The October Days

3 The abolition of feudalism

4 The ideas of leading revolutionaries

5 The aristocratic revolt

6 The failure of Louis XVI's financial reforms

← Least important          Most important →

# The attempts to establish a constitutional monarchy

REVISED

## Political, judicial and administrative reforms

Back in Paris the deputies of the National Assembly, along with the king and his court, brought forward a series of reforms aimed at removing the administrative chaos of the past.

### Political and administrative reforms

France was divided into 83 **departments** for elections and local government. These were divided into districts (547), cantons (4,872), and communes (about 44,000) which would be run by elected councils. More power was given to local areas as a safeguard against a royal recovery of power.

The right to vote was given to 'active citizens' – all men over 25 who paid a certain level of tax, around 4 million men in total. Those ineligible were the 3 million 'passive citizens'.

### Taxation

Under the new system, everyone paid. All were liable to pay the land tax and the tax on commercial profits while just 'active citizens' paid a tax on moveable goods – for example, grain.

### Judicial reforms

All previous courts were replaced by a uniform system. There was a **Justice of the Peace** in each canton, trial was by jury, and torture and mutilation were abolished. Justice was free and equal for all.

## Church reforms

The deputies passed Church reforms:
- All Church property became the property of the state.
- Abuses such as pluralism were abolished.
- The clergy were to be paid by the state instead of collecting the tithe.
- Monastic orders that provided neither education nor charitable work were suppressed.
- Protestants were given full civil rights.

The clergy accepted this, although many were unhappy that Catholicism was not made the official religion of France.

### Civil Constitution of the Clergy, 12 July 1790

Bishop's dioceses were reorganised to coincide with the 83 new departments. All other clerical posts, apart from parish priests, were removed. Appointment to any clerical post was by election. Many clergy opposed this, but their call for a Church synod was denied, so they waited for the judgement of the Pope.

### The Clerical Oath, 27 November 1790

The deputies forced the issue by requiring all clergy to take an oath to the Constitution. The Pope came out against the reforms. Over 50 per cent of clergy refused – they were called **refractory clergy** and removed from their posts. For devout Catholics like Louis, there was a clash between their religion and the revolution. As a result, a significant number of people now opposed the revolution.

## Economic and social change

The deputies believed in **laissez-faire**. All internal customs barriers were abolished, as were the guilds that regulated craft industries. The one exception was that unions were banned and strikes made illegal.

The deputies saw relief for the poor as the duty of the state. They examined the extent of the problem, almost 2 million people begging, but lacked the finance to do anything.

To finance government **assignats** were introduced, backed by the sale of Church lands. This land sale provided income, created people with a vested interest in supporting the revolution and left the clergy dependent upon the state for their salaries and thus more likely to be supporters of the new state.

**Judge for yourself** a

Read the two sources, the question and the answer provided.

Highlight the sections that refer to:

- context (and incorporate knowledge)
- provenance
- tone and emphasis.

Use your judgements to decide which level of the mark scheme this answer fits in.

> With reference to these sources and your understanding of the historical context, which of these two sources is more valuable in explaining the importance of the Clerical Oath?

Source A shows that this priest will not swear the clerical oath because it is against his religion. He is simply stating his position, but does say he would be a coward if he swore. The oath did force people to choose between their religion and the revolution and about 50 per cent of the clergy did not swear. So this source is valuable as evidence of why one priest would not. Source B comes from a decree from the Legislative Assembly so it shows us exactly what the Revolutionary Government was worried about. The revolts in the west of France, like the Vendée, did involve priests. So this source is more valuable as it gives the bigger picture.

## SOURCE A

From the declaration of the parish priest of Quesques et Lottinghem, January 1791.

I declare that my religion does not allow me to take an oath such as the National Assembly requires; I am happy and I even promise to watch over as well as one possibly can the faithful of this parish who are entrusted to me, to be true to the nation and the king and to observe the Constitution decreed by the National Assembly and sanctioned by the king in all that is within the competence of his power, in all that belongs to him in the order of purely civil and political matters, but where the government and the laws of the Church are concerned, I recognise no superior and other legislators than the pope and the bishops; you Christians would certainly not wish to be led by apostates and schismatics and I would be such a one if I had had the cowardice to take an oath such as the National Assembly requires, ...

## SOURCE B

Extracts from the decree of the Legislative Assembly, August 1792 regarding clerics who had not sworn the clerical oath.

The Legislative Assembly believes the unrest excited in the kingdom by priests who are not under oath is one of the major causes of danger to the fatherland. This comes at a time when all Frenchmen have need of unity, and of all their strength to drive back the external enemies, and must take all measures possible to ensure and guarantee peace within the nation ...

Article 1. All clergy liable to the oath prescribed by the law of December 26th 1790 and that of April 17th 1791 who have not sworn it, or who, after having sworn it, have retracted it ... will be obliged to leave the borders of their district and department of residence within eight days, and the kingdom, within a fortnight.

# Reaction to change internally and externally, part 1

## The king and the flight to Varennes

Initially Louis accepted the revolution and appeared willing to work towards a constitutional monarchy. Two problems changed his position. First was his religion; second was the realisation that, as a prisoner in Paris, his negotiating position was weak.

By 1791 it was obvious that Louis was avoiding hearing mass celebrated by clergy who had sworn the clerical oath. When the royal family tried to leave Paris in April to spend Easter at Saint Cloud, crowds blocked them in. The National Guard could not clear their way. Louis decided to escape.

On 20 June 1791 the royal family left Paris in disguise and travelled east. They were recognised and stopped at Varennes, then brought back. The Parisian crowds watched in silence. Louis had left behind a proclamation denouncing the revolution. The results showed that:

- Louis hadn't understood how popular the changes since 1789 had been
- many no longer trusted Louis
- constitutional monarchy was in doubt
- support for republicanism started to grow.

## The political clubs

As the revolution developed, people meeting together to discuss politics gradually became a series of political clubs.

### The Jacobin Club

This was a powerful political club. Its members came from the wealthier sections of society. Many were deputies and in their debates they discussed issues that arose in the National Assembly. It acted as a pressure group for revolutionary ideas. By June 1791 it had 2,400 members in Paris and a network of Jacobin clubs across France. **Robespierre** emerged as leader.

Following the flight to Varennes, radical **Jacobins** argued that Louis had in effect abdicated and should not be replaced, unless the nation disagreed. This republican manifesto split the Jacobins.

### The Cordeliers Club

This club originated in the Cordeliers district of Paris. Its members were poorer men and women and was more radical than the Jacobins. Its leadership was middle class, though – notably **Danton**, Desmoulins, Marat and **Hébert**. The Cordeliers saw their role as keeping an eye on the National Assembly deputies and as leaders of the democratic movement.

### The Club Monarchique

This was a counter-revolutionary club. Its members (around 200) included National Assembly deputies, clergy, nobles and upper bourgeoisie. It sponsored propaganda, fostered links with **émigrés** and encouraged similar clubs across France. These worked for a return to an Ancien Régime-style monarchy.

### The Feuillants

This club was set up by those who left the Jacobins when it split. Its members, many of them National Assembly deputies, supported constitutional monarchy. After the Champ de Mars massacre they took control in the National Assembly and produced the new constitution.

## The demonstration at the Champ de Mars, 17 July 1791

The Cordeliers organised a signing ceremony for a republican petition on the Champ de Mars. Roughly 50,000 people attended. The National Guard under Lafayette were called out to maintain order. They fired on the crowd – up to 50 people were killed and the rest dispersed. In the aftermath its leaders, Brissot and Danton, fled. The Cordeliers Club was shut down.

**Comparing two sources (for the AS exam only)**

Read the two sources below. Your task is to compare content, provenance and tone.

|  | Main points of the content | Observations about the provenance in terms of who? what? where? when? why? and the tone |
|---|---|---|
| Source A | | |
| Source B | | |
| Main similarities and differences | | |

You can then reach a conclusion about which you think is the more valuable for understanding the Flight to Varennes.

### SOURCE A

From a letter to the British Government written by Lord Gower in Paris, 1 July 1791.

I am going to write private truths which might be unpleasant to a royal eye. If this country ceases to be a monarchy it will be entirely the fault of Louis XVI. Blunder upon blunder, inconsequence upon inconsequence, a total want of energy of mind accompanied with personal cowardice, have been the destruction of his reign. In this last affair, when he had undertaken to escape from Paris, or if you will, to go to Montmedy, he ought to have effected his plans or perished in the attempt. It will be difficult to persuade me that he intended to stay at Montmedy, especially after the Comte D'Artois gave the émigrés in Holland hope of his brother's speedy arrival among them.

### SOURCE B

From a speech made by the Jacobin deputy Abbé Grégoire to the National Assembly, 15 July 1791.

The premier public servant abandons his post; he arms himself with a false passport; after having said, in writing to the foreign powers, that his most dangerous enemies are those who spread alleged doubts about the monarch's intentions, he breaks his word. He leaves the French a declaration which, if not criminal, is at the least – however it is envisaged – contrary to the principles of our liberty. He could not be unaware that his flight exposed the nation to the dangers of civil war; and finally, in the hypothesis that he wished only to go to Montmedy, I say: either he wanted to content himself with making peaceful observations to the National Assembly regarding its decrees, and in that case it was useless to flee; or he wanted to support his claims with arms, and in that case it was a conspiracy against liberty ...

 **Recommended reading**

Below is a list of suggested further reading on this topic.

- John Hardman, 'The real and imagined conspiracies of Louis XVI', Chapter 3 in *Conspiracy in the French Revolution*, Chapter 3 'The real and imagined conspiracies of Louis XVI' by John Hardman, pages 63–101, ed. Peter R. Campbell, Thomas E. Kaiser and Marisa Linton (2007)
- Munroe Price, *The Fall of the French Monarchy*, Chapters 8, 9 and 10, pages 169–230 (2002)
- William Doyle, *The Oxford History of the French Revolution*, second edition, Chapter 6, pages 136–58 (2012)

# Reaction to change internally and externally, part 2

## The Legislative Assembly

Under the new constitution, elections took place. On 1 October the 745 new deputies of the Legislative Assembly met. They were well off, as expected from an election system which favoured the wealthy, and were mostly from the bourgeoisie. A few were nobles, most of whom had emigrated or retired to their country estates. A few were clergy. Many distrusted the king after Varennes.

- 136 deputies were Jacobins.
- 264 deputies were Feuillants.
- 345 deputies were unaligned.

The republican Brissot and his supporters, now known as **Girondins**, seized control of the debates on refractory clergy and the émigrés, both seen as counter-revolutionary threats. Two laws were passed. One made not swearing the clerical oath a crime – conspiracy against the state. The second demanded the confiscation of the property of any émigrés, including Louis' brothers, who refused to return to France. Louis vetoed both laws, as the republicans had planned. He appeared to be obstructing the work of the Legislative Assembly. This increased his unpopularity. The Feuillants had failed to make constitutional monarchy work.

## The origins and impact of war

The other European powers, all monarchies, monitored the progress of the revolution. An attack on a fellow monarch threatened them all, but a weakened France was in their national interests. In August 1791 Austria and Prussia issued the Pillnitz Declaration, threatening combined military intervention in French affairs in support of the king, but did nothing. However, the threat and the presence of émigré troops under the Comte d'Artois, Louis' brother, on France's north-eastern frontier, made the revolutionaries even more suspicious of the monarchy. They feared counter-revolution and invasion.

### Views in France on war with Austria

| For | Against |
| --- | --- |
| • Republicans such as Brissot believed war would force Louis to reveal his true position and force traitors out into the open. | • Robespierre didn't trust the generals. He believed that France might lose. |
| • Louis believed if a war went well he, as commander in chief, might recover his powers. If it went badly, the Austrian victors would restore his old powers. | • The Feuillants regarded peace as important to preserving the gains of a revolution that had gone far enough. |
| • Marie Antoinette believed that Louis would benefit from a French defeat. | |
| • Army generals, Lafayette and Dumouriez, believed a short successful war would strengthen the authority of the king and increase their influence. | |

The pro-war groups won the argument and France declared war on Austria. Only seven deputies voted against.

The Revolutionary War began badly. Almost half the officers of the French army had become émigrés and its soldiers were demoralised. They were soon retreating, with their Generals urging peace talks. In Paris, Brissot and the Girondins were anxious to avoid any blame and accused the generals, the king and the mysterious **'Austrian Committee'** of betraying France. Lafayette visited Paris from his army and called for the Jacobin Club to be closed. The war had forced people to take sides.

**RAG – rate the timeline**

Below are a sample question and a timeline. Read the question, study the timeline and, using three coloured pens, put a red, amber or green star next to the events to show:

- red: events and policies that have no relevance to the question
- amber: events and policies that have some significance to the question
- green: events and policies that are directly relevant to the question.

1. How far was Louis XVI responsible for his own fall from power?

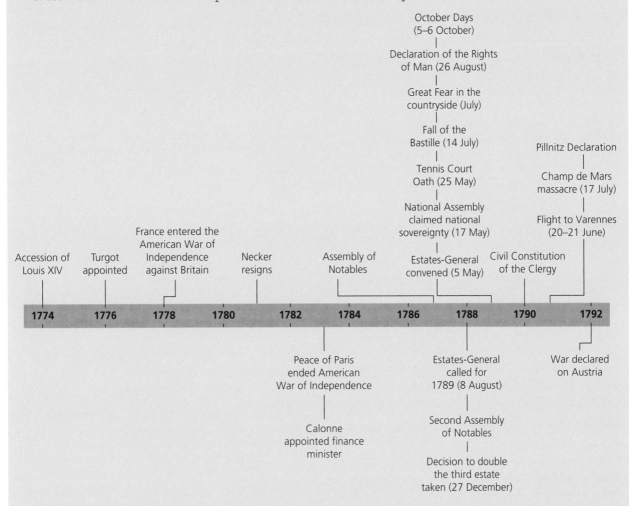

Now repeat the activity with the following questions:

2. 'The French Revolution was not so much a social conflict but more a political accident.' Explain why you agree or disagree with this view.

3. How important a factor was the decision to go to war against Britain in 1778 to the coming of the French Revolution?

4. 'The French nobility brought the French Revolution upon themselves.' Explain why you agree or disagree with this view.

 **Recommended reading**

Below is a list of suggested further reading on the outbreak of war in 1792.

- Mike Rapport, *The Napoleonic Wars: A Very Short Introduction*, Chapter 2, pages 22–26 (2013)
- William Doyle, *The Oxford History of the French Revolution*, second edition, Chapter 8, pages 174–181 (2012)

# Sans-culottes and the collapse of the constitutional experiment

## Sans-culottes

The sans-culottes had been important to the revolution from the beginning. They dominated Paris and the Paris Commune. They wanted more extreme measures than the Legislative Assembly deputies, such as food price controls and the vote. Price rises and food shortages triggered riots in early 1792 and made them more militant.

### The overthrow of the monarchy, 10 August 1792

Other events of 1792 – the war propaganda of the Girondins, the military defeats, Louis' use of his veto, his dismissal of Brissot, and Lafayette's call for the Jacobin Club to be shut down – all added to this militancy. In the journée of 20 June thousands of sans-culottes occupied the royal palace, the Tuileries, and forced Louis to wear a red cap of liberty. The end of the monarchy was in sight.

In July, following the decree of a state of emergency, provincial National Guards (**fédérés**) began to arrive in Paris, joining increased calls for the end of the monarchy. Meanwhile, Prussia's army commander threatened to destroy Paris if the royal family were harmed – this was known as the Brunswick Declaration and identified Louis with the enemy.

It is not clear who actively organised the overthrow of Louis, but it involved Danton and Robespierre. In the journée of 10 August the Tuileries was attacked and its defenders killed. The royal family took refuge with the Legislative Assembly. The deputies were then forced to hand over Louis (he was imprisoned) and to agree to a new election, by universal suffrage, of a National Convention that was to draw up a new democratic constitution for the Republic.

## The September massacres

In the aftermath, power was shared between the deputies of the Legislative Assembly, the Insurrectionist Commune who controlled Paris and a new body created by them both – the Provisional Executive Council, which was dominated by Danton. In another sign of the changed times, an Extraordinary Tribunal was set up to try those who had committed counter-revolutionary offences on 10 August and some people were guillotined.

Meanwhile, the Revolutionary War continued to go badly. The Prussians invaded. General Lafayette, after trying to march his army on Paris, defected to the Austrians. It seemed that the Prussians would capture Paris within weeks. In response, the Insurrectionist Commune ordered the arrest of hundreds of suspected counter-revolutionaries. Rumours spread that they planned to escape from prison, massacre the people and surrender Paris to the advancing Prussians. Marat and other extremists called for them to be killed. When news of the fall of Verdun reached Paris on 2 September, the prisons were broken into and over the next four days about 1,300 prisoners were murdered. The Paris Commune did nothing to stop this. The killings shocked Paris, France and the rest of Europe.

## Elections to the National Convention

Elections began in August and continued through September. All men over 21 could vote. The new National Convention met on 20 September. Meanwhile, the Prussians had been defeated at Valmy and withdrew from France. The revolution was safe for the moment.

**Mind map**

Read the question and complete the mind map to identify those people and groups who shared in the blame.

Then prioritise your reasons by adding numbers to each oval box – with 1 as the most important reason and 6 as the least important.

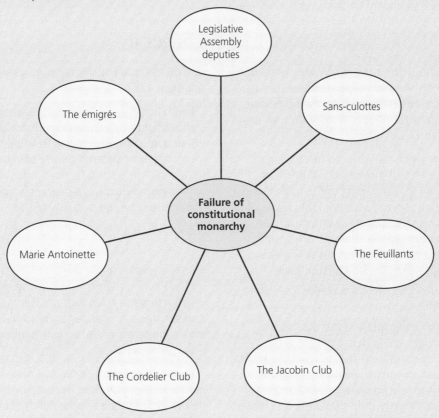

'Louis XVI was chiefly to blame for the failure of constitutional monarchy.' Explain why you agree or disagree with this view.

## Support or challenge? a

Below is a sample exam question which asks how far you agree with a specific statement. Below this is a series of general statements which are relevant to the question. Using your own knowledge and the information on the opposite page, decide whether these statements support or challenge the statement in the question.

'Violence was the driving force of the French Revolution up to the end of 1792'. How far do you agree?

| | Support | Challenge |
| --- | --- | --- |
| Louis moved troops into the Paris and Versailles area in 1789 | | |
| The garrison of the Bastille fired first on 14 July 1789 | | |
| The Brunswick Manifesto (1792) threatened vengeance on Paris | | |
| Revolutionaries were eager to declare war on Austria in 1792 | | |
| The Insurrectionist Committee organised the armed overthrow of the monarchy on 10 August 1792 | | |
| During the September Massacres 1,500 prisoners were murdered | | |

# Exam focus

On pages 39–40 is a sample answer to an AS-level question on source evaluation. Read the answer and the comments around it.

With reference to Sources A and B and your understanding of the historical context, which of these two sources is more valuable in explaining why the émigrés contributed to the failure of constitutional monarchy in the years 1789–92?

## SOURCE A

Louis XVI describes the position he was placed in when the National Assembly passed legislation against émigrés. His letter to Baron de Breteuil, his plenipotentiary for negotiations with foreign powers, is dated 14 December 1791.

The cruel law against the émigrés forced me to make use of the veto; the necessity of this has been recognised by a large part of the nation. But the men of faction, never for a moment losing sight of their aim of trying to put me in an embarrassing position, have returned the charge from another flank. ... The absurd law on émigrés was a two edged sword: if I sanctioned it I should have dishonoured myself by seeming to approve its cruel dispositions ...

They would also have exploited this sanction by saying that I only gave it to demonstrate thereby that I was not free; and from that follows the whole gamut of accusation you can easily imagine. The policy which I have laid down for myself, that of acting as freely as I can within the limits laid down by the constitution prescribed my use of my veto.

## SOURCE B

Extracts from the declaration of war on Austria, 20 April 1792.

The National Assembly, deliberating at the formal request of the king, considering that the court of Vienna, in contempt of the treaties has continued to afford open protection to French rebels, that it has instigated and formed a concert [alliance] with several European powers against the independence and security of the French nation;

That Francis I, king of Hungary and Bohemia, has refused to renounce this concert;

That he has formally infringed the sovereignty of the French nation by declaring his intention of supporting the claims of the German princes with possessions in France to whom the French nation has consistently offered compensation for their loss of feudal dues;

That he has sought to divide French citizens and arm them against each other by offering the malcontents a support in the concert of powers ...

## SOURCE C

A letter dated 25 March 1791 from George Hammond, a British diplomat in Paris, to James Burges, British under-secretary for Foreign Affairs. Hammond is reporting on the political situation in Paris.

There is no assertion of Mr Burke's more true than this – that the French have shown themselves much more skilful in destroying than in erecting. As I am convinced that no man in this country, even at this moment, has any clear notion of the new order of things that is to arise in place of the old.

No party in the National Assembly seems to be actuated by an adherence to a regular well-defined system, which is, I think, pretty clearly proved by the contradictory decrees that are every day issuing out to answer the emergency of the moment. And even if there was a system, there does not appear to be any man of abilities so transcendent, or of patriotism so unsuspected, as to be capable of giving direction and energy to the movements of any compact concentrated body of individuals.

In the meantime they avoid rendering themselves unpopular, by throwing the execution of everything that is either odious or absurd in their own numerous decrees on the king and his ministers. They have stripped royalty of everything that could make it either respectable or amiable.

From Source A and Source B we are given two perspectives on the émigrés in 1791–92. Source A focuses upon how they are being used to place the king in a difficult position. Source B, by contrast, focuses specifically on the threat to France that the émigrés represent and how they are being supported by the hated enemy, Austria. Both sources offer an insight into how the émigrés were perceived, but which is more valuable in explaining the threat to Constitutional Monarchy that they represented?

Source A is Louis XVI sharing his thinking privately with the man who acts as a go-between for him with other monarchs. This makes it an invaluable insight into his thinking. Louis is obviously trying to explain his decision to veto the law against the émigrés so when he calls the law 'cruel' and 'absurd' he is trying to make his case as strongly as possible. Clearly, not everyone in France would have thought the law absurd. The National Assembly deputies voted for this law, so many people were clearly concerned. And just because Louis sees a conspiracy against him does not necessarily mean that such a conspiracy did exist.

The context of the source is the threat posed to the revolution by the émigrés who had fled, especially Louis' brother, the Comte D'Artois, who was with the émigré army at Coblenz. In their Pillnitz Declaration, Austria and Prussia had threatened military intervention in support of Louis and this understandably aroused the suspicions of the revolutionaries. So, too, did the threats Louis' brothers had made from their courts in exile and the plots they started. The law against the émigrés effectively declared them outlawed, as they were conspiring against the revolution and it threatened them with death if caught. It also confiscated their lands and income. If Louis had agreed to the law he would have been pronouncing this sentence on his brothers, both of whom had fled from France.

While Louis is downplaying the level of the threat to the revolution the émigrés represent, it is worth remembering that he publicly demanded that the Elector of Trier disperse the émigré army, while at the same time writing privately to him asking him not to. However, Louis's claim that the émigrés are being used as an excuse to put him in a difficult position by 'men of faction' does have some truth to it. His enemies in the Legislative Assembly, republicans like Brissot, did want constitutional monarchy to fail. If they could make the king appear as obstructing the progress of the revolution by vetoing their laws then that would make him more unpopular and help them achieve what they wanted.

Source B is a valuable source. It is the formal declaration of war and states exactly what the reasons for this are and this includes that the Austrians are offering the émigrés protection and arming them. When the Legislative Assembly voted for war only seven out of 745 deputies did not support it.

The context of the source is the state of France in 1791, the struggle over how the country should be governed and what powers the king should have as a constitutional monarch. There was growing distrust between the king on one side and the revolutionaries on the other side, including the growing strength of republicanism. The activities of the émigrés outside France, who were committed to overthrowing the revolution, contributed to this and Louis had tried to stop them undermining his position. Inside France there were counter-revolutionary groups, like the Club Monarchique and the Amis du Roi, who were in contact with the émigrés, too. The threat that the émigrés represented, coupled with the Pillnitz Declaration, is made very clear to the historian in the declaration of war. They are mentioned twice and the Austrian monarch is accused

The opening paragraph sets up the contrast between the two sources. Perhaps something should have been said about the evaluation of the sources, rather than simply describing their basic content.

There is some good analysis here. The candidate realises that the source has flaws and spells out some of the flaws.

A pretty good attempt to put the source into context using knowledge.

Good use of contextual knowledge displayed in this paragraph – though not fully linked to the 'value' of the source.

This paragraph is short and concise. There is nothing wrong with that. Good focus on the purpose of the source and excellent use of contextual knowledge although not explicitly applied to the value of the source.

Good use of knowledge in this paragraph. Moreover, it is reasonably linked to the 'value' of the source.

of helping them and entering into alliances with others, notably Prussia, to threaten the 'security of the French nation'. What they mean by this is threatening the revolution – another clue to this is the reference to Austria's support of German princes, who had lands in France in which they had lost their feudal rights.

Source B, however, does not offer any help to the historian on the other reasons why the republicans who dominated the Legislative Assembly wanted to go to war against Austria – that is, that Brissot and his followers believed that war would force people to choose and that it would bring traitors out into the open. That fits with their other plans that Louis refers to in Source A of trying to discredit the king. Having said that, Source B is more valuable as it captures the view of the leading revolutionaries in the Legislative Assembly on the problem of the émigrés, while Source A offers only an insight into the views of one man, even though he was a very important man.

The conclusion is sensible. It makes the crucial point that a source from an individual viewpoint has its limits, even if that individual is a key player in events. However, the balance between content and provenance could be improved. There is too much content and not enough provenance.

This is a high Level 4 answer. The sources are interpreted with confidence and the essay reaches a judgement based on the interpretations of the sources and own knowledge. However, the essay could say more about the tone and provenance of the sources. The conclusion is largely about content – and it shouldn't be!

### What makes a good answer?

List the characteristics of a good source-based essay, using the examples and comments above.

# Exam focus

Below is a sample Level 5 answer to an A-level question on source evaluation. Read the answer and the comments around it.

With reference to Sources A, B and C (see page 38) and your understanding of the historical context, assess the value of these three sources to an historian studying the constitutional monarchy experiment 1789–92.

Source A is a letter written by Louis XVI to his plenipotentiary for negotiations with foreign powers. It is valuable to a historian, as it is Louis sharing his private thoughts with one of his key supporters, one of the men who had to represent him to other monarchs. Louis is one of the key figures in this period and knowing what he thought about such crucial matters as the issue of how to deal with the émigrés is important. Clearly his use of loaded language, describing the law as 'cruel' and 'absurd', gives away his position, and his suggestion that people are deliberately putting him in a difficult position would require corroboration, as would his argument that he would be in the wrong whether he had vetoed the law or not. But to know what he was privately thinking is invaluable.

> This is a pretty good introduction, which analyses some of the main aspects of the source, particularly provenance.

The letter was written after Louis had vetoed the law against the émigrés. Undoubtedly at the time they posed a serious threat to the revolution as is evidenced by the Legislative Assembly voting for the law. There was an émigré army, led by Louis' brother, the Comte D'Artois, at Coblenz, which had Austrian support. In their Pillnitz Declaration, Austria and Prussia had threatened military intervention in support of Louis and there had been a number of threats and plots coming from his brothers' courts in exile. Seen in that light, a law which effectively declared the émigrés outlaws and declared their lands and revenues forfeit and their lives, too, if they were captured, might not have seemed 'cruel' to many in France. Of course, this is a personal view but shows Louis' sympathies are with the émigrés, his supporters.

> Good use of contextual knowledge displayed.

While Louis is downplaying the level of the threat to the revolution the émigrés represent, it is worth remembering that he publicly demanded that the Elector of Trier disperse the émigré army, while at the same time writing privately to him asking him not to. This letter reinforces the view that the revolutionaries were right to not trust the king. What is more valuable in the source is Louis' claim that the émigrés are being used as an excuse to put him in a difficult position by 'men of faction'. His enemies in the Legislative Assembly, republicans like Brissot, did not want constitutional monarchy to succeed. If they could make the king appear as obstructing the progress of the revolution by vetoing their laws then that would make him more unpopular and help them achieve what they wanted. The letter reveals that Louis was aware of this – and if he was, then others would be too. One final point is that Louis defends himself by saying his policy is one of acting as 'freely as I can within the limits laid down by the constitution'. This is helpful to the historian trying to decide if Louis did really plan to become a constitutional monarch or whether, as some historians argue, he was only looking for a way to regain as much power as possible.

> By this point the answer is becoming a little speculative but nevertheless does pick up on the content and tone.

Source B is a valuable source. It is the formal declaration of war and states exactly what the reasons for this are – the Austrians are arming and protecting the French émigrés, supporting those German princes with lands in France who have lost their feudal rights (a clear signal that they are against that key gain of the revolution) and threatening the national security of France. The émigrés are variously referred to as 'rebels' and 'malcontents' and all the blame is placed upon the Austrians having 'instigated' and 'infringed'. The fact that this declaration of war was passed in the Legislative Assembly by a vote where only seven of the 745 deputies did not support it shows that this source captures the thinking of those deputies who, in turn, represented the revolution.

A clear start to analysing Source B.

However, while the source captures the public reasons for a declaration of war, the situation in France was more complicated. Yes, the émigrés were a threat and yes, Austria did threaten the revolution, but some of the leading French politicians had other motives, too. The king thought that whatever the outcome of war, he would benefit. If France won then Louis, as commander in chief, might regain some of his powers and if France lost then the Austrians might restore him to his old position. The queen was convinced that France would lose and that her countrymen, the Austrians, would help restore Louis' power. In fact she went so far as to help them by sending details of French plans in her secret correspondence.

Good use of contextual knowledge in this paragraph, although losing focus on the question towards the end.

Some deputies, the Feuillants, were against the war. They, too, thought France might lose and they believed that the revolution had gone far enough and wanted to protect its gains. More importantly, this source does not reveal the motives of those like Brissot and the Girondins who wanted a war, as they believed it would force traitors out into the open. It was they who steered the Legislative Assembly to vote for war. Among these traitors they suspected Louis and the queen and the shadowy Austrian Committee. So the source is valuable in terms of what it actually says, but also limited in terms of the motives that are not shown and the complexity of the political debate over the working of constitutional monarchy that was taking place in France.

Again, good use of knowledge of the context – and here it is more effectively linked to the 'value' of the source.

Source C comes from a British diplomat reporting back to the British Government. This can be viewed as a neutral outsider looking at the situation, but the tone of the writer is critical of the French, saying that they are more 'skilful in destroying than erecting'. Also, when he says that no one knows what the new order may look like, that is not strictly true. Some Frenchmen had a very clear idea what sort of political system they wanted. For example, the Feuillants wanted a working constitutional monarchy, while the Jacobins wanted it to fail and already republicanism was gaining ground.

The candidate makes a useful point about the value of outsider testimony and backs this up with their contextual knowledge. They might have expanded on that a little.

However, the source is very valuable in learning the British opinion of the leading French politicians. Hammond does not appear to rate any of them very highly. This is useful to know. And what Source C also notes is that the revolutionaries are throwing the blame for anything bad or unpopular onto the king. As an outsider, Hammond has spotted this tendency but he appears to be unaware of the motives of Brissot and the revolutionaries, which Louis himself referred to in Source A – their attempt to discredit the monarchy in order to remove it. So, Source A is clearly most valuable and Source C least valuable.

Mature level of English assists the clarity of the argument.

This is a very strong response with confident and appropriate knowledge of the context deployed to assess the value of the sources. The assessment of Sources A and C is especially impressive, commenting on the status of the authors and the content of the sources. The assessment of Source B, while strong in the deployment of own knowledge, is less effective in relation to the provenance of the source. Too much knowledge gets in the way of the analysis. This is a Level 5 response, but two points should be noted: the introduction is general and adds little; and the conclusion, while thoughtful, is not necessary as there is no requirement for comparative assessment in the question.

**What makes a good answer?**

List the characteristics of a good source-based essay, using the examples and comments above.

## The establishment of a republic

### Problems and policies

The 749 new deputies of the National Convention were mostly lawyers, professional men and property owners. Numbers of nobles and clergy were lower than ever, but for the first time there were a few artisans. Their first decision was a unanimous vote to abolish the monarchy.

### Girondins versus Jacobins/Montagnards

There was a clear division among the deputies. Seated together on the high benches on the left-hand side of the hall where the deputies met were those who came to be known as Montagnards, from 'the Mountain' where they sat. Opposing them were those on the right, who came to be known as Girondins. Both groups were members of the Jacobin club. In between, on the lower benches or the 'Plain', sat the main group of uncommitted deputies. From the beginning, the Girondins and Montagnards fought political battles over the conduct of the war, how to deal with the king and over their personal antagonisms. The Girondins accused the Montagnards of wanting to impose a political dictatorship and of being responsible for the September massacres. They were also hostile to the popular radicalism of the sans-culottes, who stood behind the Montagnards.

### The debate leading to the execution of the king

With the monarchy abolished, the next question was what to do with Louis. The Girondins wanted a trial and to hold Louis as a hostage for possible future use in negotiations with the Austrians and Prussians. The Montagnards viewed him as already guilty of treason and wanted him punished. The Girondins won the argument and persuaded the deputies of the National Convention to agree to try Louis.

The verdict was never in any doubt, especially after a workman discovered the armoire de fer at the Tuileries in November 1792. This was an iron wall safe which contained correspondence between Louis and the Austrians, along with other compromising documents. Despite this further evidence of Louis plotting with foreign powers, the sentence remained in doubt. Once again the two factions clashed.

Robespierre and the Montagnards argued for the death penalty, while the Girondins wanted the sentence to be subject to a referendum of the people. They believed the people of the provinces, unlike the people of Paris, would not want Louis' death. But their efforts failed. At Marat's suggestion the deputies had to declare their decision publicly. Louis was found guilty. When it came to deciding on the sentence, 387 voted for the death penalty and 288 voted for imprisonment. On 21 January 1793 he was guillotined.

> ## The successive legislative assemblies of the revolution
>
> The Estates-General became:
> - National (Constituent) Assembly 1789–September 1791
> - Legislative Assembly October 1791–September 1792
> - National Convention September 1792–October 1795.

## ! Delete as applicable a

Below are a sample exam question and a paragraph written in answer to this question. Read the paragraph and decide which of the possible options (in bold) is most appropriate. Delete the least appropriate options and complete the paragraph by justifying your selection.

How successful were the Girondins in the National Convention in managing the trial of Louis XVI?

The Girondins in the National Convention were successful to a **great/fair/limited** extent. For example, they persuaded the deputies to hold a trial. The Montagnards viewed him as guilty already and believed a trial was unnecessary. The Girondins were also successful in getting a conviction. However, they wanted to keep Louis as a bargaining chip and didn't want the sentence to be death. In this respect they were outmanoeuvred by the Montagnards, who ensured that the deputies had to publicly cast their vote on what sentence to give, imprisonment or death. In this way, the Girondins in the National Assembly were **extremely/moderately/slightly/not** successful because

_____

_____

## ⊕ Identify the tone and emphasis of a source

Study the source below. Focus on the:

- language
- sentence structure
- emphasis of the source
- overall tone.

What does the tone and emphasis of the source suggest about its value in terms of the:

- reliability of the evidence
- utility of the evidence for studying attitudes towards Louis XVI's trial and sentence?

### SOURCE A

From a letter by George Monro to Lord Grenville, British Foreign Secretary, 21 January 1793.

I am sorry it has fallen to be my lot to be the messenger of the most disagreeable intelligence, that I, or any one else was perhaps ever obliged to communicate. The National Convention after sitting near thirty-four hours on Thursday night, voted that the punishment of death should be inflicted upon His Most Christian Majesty. This unjust, and iniquitous judgement was carried by a majority of rather more than a hundred; fifty of this number, though they voted for death, differed in opinion from the rest in respect to the time it should be inflicted; some thinking it should not be put into execution till the war was finished, and others proposing it should be postponed, til the vote of the people was taken.

## The spread of the Revolutionary War 1793

At the end of 1792 the Revolutionary War had been going well for France, but this ended in early 1793 when the First Coalition was formed. France was attacked on all sides.

### First Coalition members

The First Coalition consisted of:
- Austria
- Britain
- Holland
- Portugal
- Prussia
- Sardinia
- Spain.

Soon British, Austrian and Spanish troops were on French soil. There were fears that the Austrians would march on Paris.

## Attempts to establish wartime control

In early 1793 the deputies of the National Convention set up two committees.

### The Committee of Public Safety

The **Committee of Public Safety (CPS)** was created to co-ordinate the war effort on 6 April 1793, two days after General Dumouriez had failed in his attempt to overthrow the National Convention. Its nine members were elected monthly by the Convention. Their function was to:
- meet in secret
- supervise the activities of all ministers and agents of the government
- pass decrees collectively relating to 'general defence, external and internal'
- report weekly to the Convention.

It was a war cabinet initially dominated by Danton. Robespierre declined to be elected at the start, thinking it had little usefulness. Carnot, responsible for war strategy and personnel, was behind the decree of 23 August that ordered the levée en masse, **conscription**. The CPS also dispatched **representatives on mission** to the armies to improve morale and supervise the generals. The defections of Dumouriez and Lafayette to the Austrians meant other generals were not trusted. Between 1793 and 1794, 84 generals were guillotined or shot and 352 were dismissed.

## The Committee of General Security

The **Committee of General Security (CGS)** was composed of 12 deputies. Their function was to:
- oversee state security, including police
- prosecute foreign agents and counterfeiters of assignats
- report regularly to the National Convention.

## The rising in the Vendée

The introduction of conscription in March 1793 triggered a revolt in the Vendée in western France. From its small beginnings in riots and **guerrilla warfare**, this escalated into open war. By the end of March an army of 20,000 rebels controlled the Vendée and had sacked several cities. The rebels were against the revolution and motivated by a mixture of:
- Royalism
- resistance to conscription
- loyalty to the Catholic Church
- local loyalties.

The CPS viewed defeating the rebels as crucial to the survival of the revolution. Extra troops were deployed. By the end of the year the rebel armies had been defeated. In the aftermath, thousands were imprisoned and tried by military commissions. Over 8,700 people were executed. Many were guillotined or shot by firing squads and others were drowned in the River Loire. Such brutality ensured that guerrilla attacks and **scorched earth** reprisals continued into 1794. By the end of the revolt as many as 200,000 people had died.

## ⚬ Identify the tone and emphasis of a source

Study the source below. Don't focus on the content – instead, focus on the:

- language
- sentence structure
- emphasis of the source
- overall tone.

What does the tone and emphasis of the source suggest about its value, in terms of the:

- reliability of the evidence
- utility of the evidence for studying attitudes towards the rebels in the Vendée?

### SOURCE A

From a letter to the minister of war by General Turreau, commander of the revolutionary armies in the Vendée, 19 January 1794.

My purpose is to burn everything, to leave nothing but what is essential to establish the necessary quarters for exterminating the rebels. This great measure is one which you should prescribe. You should also make an advance statement as to the fate of the women and children we will come across in this rebellious countryside. If they are all to be put to the sword, I cannot undertake such action without authorisation.

All brigands caught bearing arms, or convicted of having taken up arms to revolt against their country, will be bayoneted. The same will apply to girls, women and children in the same circumstances. Those who are merely under suspicion will not be spared either, but no execution may be carried out except by previous order of the general.

## ⓘ Introducing and concluding an argument

Look at the key points of the answer.

- How good is the proposed introduction?
- How effective is the proposed conclusion?
- Could either be improved – especially in relation to Level 5 answers?

How successful was the Committee of Public Safety in ensuring that France was able to successfully wage war in the years 1792–1795?

**Key points:**

- Individual members of the CPS took responsibility for different aspects of the war effort.
- The economy was controlled to develop war industries.
- Conscription produced a great army.
- The CPS dispatched representatives on mission to the armies.

**Introduction:**

France won the Revolutionary War that ended in 1795. It was able to do so because of the efforts of the Committee of Public Safety. Carnot was the member responsible for war strategy and personnel and in later years he was regarded as the architect of victory. That is why after Thermidor he did not die with Robespierre. Other members also contributed to winning the war. However, it should also be remembered that France's enemies did not work together being more interested in their own aims and that too contributed to their defeat.

**Conclusion:**

In conclusion, the Committee of Public Safety was successful in ensuring that France could win the war.

# Internal and external war, part 2

## Maximilien Robespierre

Robespierre first came to national attention in 1789 when he was elected as a deputy to the Estates-General. He became well known for his Jacobin views, his belief in democracy and his opposition to capital punishment and slavery. He was greatly influenced by the ideas of Rousseau. Robespierre rose to prominence in the Jacobin Club and gained a reputation as an incorruptible politician. In August 1792 he was elected to the National Convention and became a leader of the Montagnard faction.

## The fall of the Girondins

The political war between the Girondins and the Montagnards continued after Louis XVI's execution. In 1793 the Girondins were unpopular for promoting the war and were blamed for its negative economic impact, especially a fall in the value of assignats which made food more expensive. The san-culottes called for price controls on basic commodities but the National Convention refused. There were disturbances in Paris in February over prices, which the National Guard brought under control.

The Girondins had support in the provinces, where the policies of leading Montagnards like Robespierre and Marat were viewed as too extreme, but not in Paris. There, sans-culottes saw the Montagnards as realists willing to take the harsh measures required to protect the revolution. The Girondins, on the other hand, attacked the sans-culottes as buveurs de sang (drinkers of blood).

In April the Girondins impeached Marat but he was acquitted by the Revolutionary Tribunal. On 1 May thousands of his sans-culotte supporters surrounded the National Convention demanding bread price controls. The next day a law setting a maximum price for grain and bread was passed.

## The Journée of 2 June 1793

At the Jacobin Club Robespierre called for an insurrection against 'corrupt deputies'. The Montagnards had allied themselves with the sans-culottes. On 2 June the National Convention was surrounded by National Guards demanding the arrest of 29 Girondins. The deputies were forced to agree. They stayed in control, with power in the hands of the Montagnards, but at the price of relying on sans-culotte power and accepting the use of armed force.

## The Federalist revolt

In response, other cities – Avignon, Bordeaux, Caen, Lyons, Marseilles and Toulon – revolted. Their motives were a mix of resentment of the influence of the Paris Commune on the course of the revolution and support for the Girondins. In time, the character of these revolts changed to counter-revolution in Lyons and Toulon.

Though a significant threat to the revolution, these cities were never able to work together. This enabled the French army to defeat and capture each of them by October.

In the aftermath representatives on mission were responsible for administering revolutionary justice. An example was made of Lyons, where Georges-Auguste Couthon executed 113 rebels in six weeks. This was not enough for the CPS. He was replaced in November by Collot d'Herbois and **Joseph Fouché**. Their revolutionary commission sentenced 1,673 people to death. To speed up the process, and to shock the local population, in December prisoners were placed in front of cannons and mown down by **grapeshot**.

## (!) Spot the mistake

**a**

Below are a sample exam question and a paragraph written in answer to this question. Why does this paragraph not get high praise? What is wrong with the focus of the answer in this paragraph?

How dangerous was the Federalist revolt to the Revolution in the months May to October 1793?

The Federalist revolt took place in the cities of Bordeaux, Lyon, Marseille and Toulon. They resented the influence of the Paris Commune on the revolution and wanted a bigger say in their own affairs. They were unhappy about the purging of the Girondin deputies, many of whom came from that region.

## (i) Turning assertion into argument

**a**

Below are a series of definitions, a sample exam question and two sample conclusions. One conclusion achieves a high mark because it contains an argument. The other achieves a lower mark because it is contains only description and assertion. Which is which? The A-level mark scheme on page 7 will help you.

- **Description:** a detailed account
- **Assertion:** a statement of fact or an opinion which is not supported by a reason
- **Reason:** a statement which explains or justifies something
- **Argument:** an assertion justified with a reason

To what extent was Robespierre the most influential revolutionary in the years 1789–94?

In the early years Robespierre was a minor figure, but he made a number of key interventions which had a great impact on the course of the Revolution. He came up with the idea of the Self-denying Ordinance which meant that when the Legislative Assembly met in 1791, those who wanted constitutional monarchy to fail could make sure it did. He was also an important member of the Insurrectionist Committee that overthrew the monarchy. Robespierre became the most influential revolutionary during the early years of the Republic because it was he who explained its key ideas, such as the relationship between virtue and terror. He was the voice of the Committee of Public Safety in the National Convention and arguably its leading figure during the crucial period when the revolution was threatened by internal revolts and external attack, as he was responsible for major policy strategy and the political police.

In conclusion, Robespierre was an influential revolutionary. He sat as a deputy in the Estates-General and became a member of the Committee of Public Safety. He was popular with the sans-culottes and the Jacobin Club. He gained a reputation as incorruptible. He was blamed for the Terror after Thermidor, but that is not fair. Nor was he a dictator, as he turned up on that last day in the National Assembly armed with nothing more than a speech.

# The progress of the war

## The progress of the Revolutionary War, 1793–94

By September 1793 the war was going in France's favour. The First Coalition members pursued their own ends rather than co-operating, and the measures taken by the Committee of Public Safety (CPS) enabled France to win.

In October the Austrians were driven out. In December Toulon was recaptured and the British fleet expelled. In the Netherlands a decisive victory was won at Fleurus on 26 June 1794. France then went on the offensive until all their opponents were knocked out of the war.

## Levée en masse

Carnot was the CPS member responsible for war strategy and personnel. He was behind the decree of 23 August that ordered the levée en masse, conscription. This produced an army of 800,000 men by 1794. The CPS put France on a war footing, with men drawn into massively expanded industries of industry, food production and transport. Women were to staff hospitals and make clothes. Government control of the economy for war made victory possible.

## The coming of the Terror

The grain price controls imposed by the National Convention in May 1793 backfired. They led to a growth in a black market for grain. Grain supplies fell and food prices rose. Further measures making hoarding grain a capital offence did not work either.

Extremists in Paris, the **Enrages**, called for higher taxes on the rich, death for hoarders and the arrest of political suspects. Again, the National Convention was surrounded by demonstrators with these demands along with the formation of a sans-culotte revolutionary army. The deputies agreed. A force of 7,000 men was set up, which was copied across France. Finally a general maximum was passed, which enforced wage and price controls throughout France.

Added to the threats of external war, internal revolt and sans-culotte power, the National Convention deputies faced a fourth, personal attack. In 1793 two revolutionaries, Lepeletier and Marat, were assassinated. In response, Terror was the 'order of the day'.

## Political Terror

The National Convention passed the Law of Suspects on 17 September 1793. This widened the definition of who was against the Revolution to include royalists, federalists, relations of émigrés and anyone without a certificate of **civisme** from their local watch committee. The watch committee were to arrest these suspects and send details of the charge to the Committee of General Security. Prison numbers rose and the Paris Revolutionary Tribunal was divided into four sections, with two sitting at any one time, to speed up the process of trying them all.

## Executions

The pace of convictions and executions increased. Between March and September 1793, 70 people were guillotined in Paris. Between October and December this rose to 178. Elsewhere, the worst atrocities of the Terror occurred in the suppression of the Vendée and federalist revolts.

## Religious Terror

**Dechristianisation**, the 'religious terror', spread across France by early 1794. This was driven by the sans-culottes, the revolutionary armies and some **representatives on mission** such as Fouché, rather than the National Convention. Revolutionary hatred of the Catholic Church led to the removal of thousands of priests and the closure of churches.

# RAG – rate the timeline

Below are a sample exam question and a timeline. Read the question, study the timeline and, using three coloured pens, put a red, amber or green star next to the events to show:

● red: events and policies that have no relevance to the question

● amber: events and policies that have some significance to the question

● green: events and policies that are directly relevant to the question.

How successful were the Committee of Public Safety in defending the revolution from its internal and external enemies between 1792 and 1795?

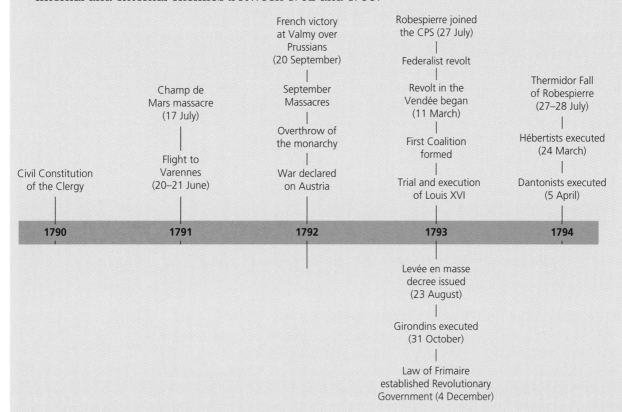

Now repeat the task with the two questions below.

'The main threat to the revolution in the period 1791 to 1795 was from foreign invasion.' Explain why you agree or disagree with this view.

How influential were the sans-culottes on the course of the revolution between 1791 and 1795?

# Recommended reading

Below is a list of suggested further reading on this topic.

● Hugh Gough, *The Terror in the French Revolution*, second edition, pages 27–37 (2010)

● Peter Jones, *The French Revolution*, second edition, pages 66–69 (2010)

● William Doyle, *The French Revolution: A Very Short Introduction*, pages 52–56 (2001)

# The spread of the Terror, part 1

## The influence of Robespierre and the sans-culottes

The trial of 21 Girondins began on 24 October 1793. They still enjoyed some support and as their trial carried on over five days an acquittal began to look likely. Robespierre intervened. He convinced the National Convention deputies to vote to speed up of trials. If after three days a jury were convinced that the accused were guilty then they could return a guilty verdict straight away. The Girondins were convicted and guillotined on 31 October. Other prominent revolutionaries followed them.

## The Dictatorship of the Committee of Public Safety

By the end of 1793 the Jacobin Government had succeeded. Revolts had been defeated and foreign troops driven from France. It was then possible for the CPS to control the sans-culottes. In September the National Convention decreed that the sections of the Paris Commune should only meet twice a week. This limited sans-culotte ability to organise. In October the deputies passed a decree that suspended the constitution with its one man one vote.

## The Law of Frimaire, 4 December 1793

This established Revolutionary Government. This:

- confirmed that the CGS and the CPS had full executive powers, including control of local government, which enabled them to break the power of the sans-culottes in the Paris Commune
- disbanded all revolutionary armies except that in Paris
- went back on all the earlier revolutionary ideals of decentralisation of government, the separation of the legislative and the executive, and the provision of impartial justice.

This Jacobin government was a dictatorship.

## Challenges to the Committee of Public Safety

In 1794 the CPS faced two challenges. The **Indulgents**, a faction led by Danton, campaigned to end to the Terror. The mood in Paris had changed and Robespierre seemed to be siding with the Indulgents. A **clemency** committee was set up. The Hébertists, followers of Hébert who wanted more Terror, were arrested. At this point Collot d'Herbois rushed back to Paris to answer criticism of his harsh repression in Lyons. He argued that a continuation of terror was needed, condemned the arrest of the Hébertists and challenged the idea of clemency. Robespierre immediately withdrew his support. He viewed both factions as threats.

In February the Hébertists were released. They accused both the Indulgents and the CPS of betraying the revolution and called for a popular rising – which didn't happen. Instead, they were rearrested and accused of plotting to betray France to its enemies. Though this was untrue, they were convicted and guillotined. The CPS disbanded the Paris revolutionary army and closed the clubs where the sans-culottes met. Hébert's supporters on the Paris Commune were replaced by Robespierre's.

The Indulgents were more of a threat because of Danton's popularity. Initially Robespierre did not want to move against them. They were arrested and accused of conspiring to overthrow the CPS and the CGS. Danton was so successful in defending himself that, fearing an acquittal, the CPS rushed through a new decree that anyone who insulted the justice system could be removed from court. The Indulgents were then removed, convicted and guillotined next day, 5 April 1794.

# Comparing two alternative answers

Read the two sources, the question and the parts of two answers.

Which answer is better for studying the value of each source? Both have begun by considering provenance and tone.

> With reference to these sources and your understanding of the historical context, which of these two sources is more valuable in explaining the Terror?

Source A is more valuable. It is the words of Robespierre himself speaking in the Convention and this would have been recorded and published afterwards. He tells the deputies why the Terror is necessary by linking it with virtue. He says 'virtue without terror is powerless', they have to fight all their enemies, those in France and those abroad. Source B is an eyewitness of the Terror but he is appears to be against the Terror. He uses phrases like 'derisively' and 'for the sake of appearances'.

Source B is more valuable, as the writer was in Paris and is describing to his brother how people were tried in batches and guillotined on the same day. Source A is Robespierre trying to justify the Terror but doesn't really give any detail about how it worked.

## SOURCE A

From a speech by Robespierre to the National Convention, 5 February 1794. In it he justified the Terror.

If the mainspring of popular government in peacetime is virtue, the mainspring of popular government in revolution is virtue and terror both: virtue, without which terror is disastrous; terror, without which virtue is powerless. Terror is nothing but prompt, severe, inflexible justice; it is therefore an emanation of virtue; it is not so much a specific principle as a consequence of the general principle of democracy applied to the homeland's most pressing needs.

## SOURCE B

From Nicolas Ruault's *Gazette of a Parisian under the Revolution*. This was based upon the letters he wrote to his brother from Paris between 1783 and 1796. Here he describes to his brother the workings of the Revolutionary Tribunal.

In the evening, prisoners at the Conciergerie are informed by a kind of extract from the indictment which warns them they are to appear before the Tribunal the next day. Indeed, they appear in numbers of fifty, sixty or seventy, seated on a rostrum of five or six rows. There they are asked their name, their age, their status, occupation, etc. … The indictment is then read to them as a group or in common. For the sake of appearances a few questions are asked of a few defendants who either reply or do not. The jury then deliberates in a small room where they remain about an hour talking among themselves, in order to do what they derisively call *deliberate*. They return to the hearing and declare *on their honour and their conscience* the defendants guilty. In two or three hours more than sixty to seventy people are thus condemned to death and executed the same day on the same scaffold.

# The spread of the Terror, part 2

## The Great Terror

During the Great Terror, 10 June to 27 July, the revolutionaries saw conspiracy everywhere. Following Danton's fall no one dared challenge the CPS. Its 11 surviving members carried on with centralising control and repression. They passed new laws.

## The Law on General Police

This law banned former nobles and foreigners from living in ports and frontier towns. It allowed the CPS to set up a police bureau to catch counter-revolutionaries and to recruit agents to identify suspects all over France. This was run by Saint-Just and later Robespierre. It sent suspects, mostly nobles and clergy suspected of counter-revolutionary conspiracy and ex-Hérbertists, to the Revolutionary Tribunal.

## Paris Revolutionary Tribunal

This was given jurisdiction over all counter-revolutionary offences by the Law of 19 Floréal. Most other revolutionary courts were shut down.

## The Law of Prairial, 10 June 1794

- Drafted by Robespierre and Couthon.
- Widened the definition of political crimes so that almost anyone could be included.
- Made guilty verdicts more likely as it abolished both defence counsels and public cross-examination of defendants. Defence witnesses did not have to be heard. Guilt could be decided by jurors rather than by any evidence produced.
- The only verdicts the Tribunal could reach were death or acquittal.
- The acquittal rate dropped to 20 per cent while the use of batch trials, groups of defendants tried together on the same charge, speeded things up.
- The numbers of people guillotined rose sharply.

## Robespierre's fall and the collapse of the Terror

The Terror came to an abrupt end in the bloodbath of Thermidor in July 1794. Robespierre tried to address the National Convention but was shouted down. The day before his arrest, Robespierre, in a long speech, had said there was a 'conspiracy against public liberty' that involved deputies, the CGS and even members of the CPS. He promised to name them. Moderates and terrorists alike feared it might be them, so they combined against Robespierre, accusing him of dictatorship.

Robespierre and his close associates on the CPS, Couthon and Saint Just, were arrested. Later that day they escaped and went to the Paris Commune to try and rally their supporters against those of the National Convention. They failed and were rearrested. Now Robespierre and his supporters, including the entire Paris Commune, had become armed rebels. That afternoon, after simply being identified, they were guillotined.

Robespierre fell because he had:
- been ill and had withdrawn from the CPS and the National Convention
- quarrelled with other CPS members, moderates and extremists, and with members of the CGS
- long-standing quarrels with the supporters of dechristianisation and the terrorists among the representatives on mission, notably Fouché
- become a figure of ridicule over his recent role as high priest of the Cult of the Supreme Being; while Robespierre officiated as High Priest the deputies behind him sniggered and made sarcastic comments about his role.
- lost sans-culotte support because of his attacks on the Hébertists and threatened wage reductions
- given other revolutionaries reason to fear that he might accuse them of conspiracy.

After Thermidor the surviving members of the CPS tried to continue the Terror, but the deputies of the National Convention reasserted their control to end it.

**Identify relevant content**

Read the following source and the question.

Go through the source and highlight the sections that are relevant for the focus of the question, and annotate in the margin the main points.

How valuable is the source for explaining why Robespierre fell?

## SOURCE A

From Nicolas Ruault's *Gazette of a Parisian under the Revolution*. This was based upon the letters he wrote to his brother between 1783 and 1796. Here he describes to his brother the events of Thermidor.

Since the death of Danton, discord has reigned in the Committee of Public Safety; Billaud-Varenne, Collot d'Herbois and Barère were together on one side, and on the other were Robespierre, Couthon, Le Bas and Saint-Just. Robespierre, who had a tendency to dominate his colleagues in the Committee and the Convention, and who aimed at a dictatorship, had completely isolated himself from them, but was nevertheless supported in his absence by Couthon and Saint-Just …

Robespierre did an about turn and on the 8th [Thermidor, 27 July] of this month in the National Convention gave a long, hypocritical speech, apologetic about his person, full of blame for a few members of the Committees of Public Safety and General Security, mixed with bitter reflections against a great number of other members, a speech in which he treated as an atrocious calumny the project attributed to him to aspire to a dictatorship, a speech which, finally, revolted the whole Convention and which he read that very evening to the Jacobins where he excited the most violent agitation for and against its author.

The members of the Convention attacked in this speech, numbering eleven, spied on by Robespierre's agents and threatened with the guillotine, gathered on the evening of the 8th in the gardens of the Tuileries and resolved to attack Robespierre during the session of the next day, the 9th, and to overthrow the kind of ideal throne on which he had placed himself. They did not fail; …

 **Recommended reading**

Below is a list of suggested further reading on this topic.

- Hugh Gough, *The Terror in the French Revolution*, second edition, pages 95–101 (2010)
- Ruth Scurr, *Fatal Purity: Robespierre and the French Revolution*, pages 295–325 (2006)
- William Doyle, *The Oxford History of the French Revolution*, second edition, pages 275–281 (2012)

# Exam focus

Below is a sample Level 5 essay. It was written in response to an AS-level question.

'Robespierre was responsible for the Terror in 1793 and 1794.' Explain why you agree or disagree with this view.

After his overthrow at Thermidor, Robespierre was blamed for the Terror. He did argue the case for Terror in the National Convention but to just blame him, one man, is an over-simplification of what happened. He must share some of the responsibility, but others were responsible too and there were limits to what he could do.

Robespierre was very influential in the Jacobin Club and in the National Convention, where he sat as a deputy among the Montagnard faction, who looked to him for leadership. In the Convention he argued for the death penalty for the king and persuaded the deputies not to do what the Girondins wanted, to keep him alive as a hostage. The execution of Louis could be seen as the start of the Terror, although some historians would point to the September massacres as a better starting point. So Robespierre, as a leading revolutionary, is responsible.

It was Robespierre who called for the journée of 2 June that led to the arrest of the Girondins and later that year in October, when their trial had gone on for five days and it looked like they might be acquitted, it was Robespierre who persuaded the National Convention deputies to speed up trials. The Girondins were then convicted and guillotined. Robespierre also made his famous speech to the Convention, justifying Terror. He was the member of the Committee of Public Safety charged with liaison with the National Convention – so was he leading it or just acting as its spokesman? This is a difficult question, as historians do not really fully understand the working of the Committee of Public Safety (CPS).

Where Robespierre can really be seen as responsible for the Terror is in his role as a member of the CPS. He ran the police bureau, with its network of spies that arrested suspected counter-revolutionaries and sent them to the Revolutionary Tribunal. His signature was on the arrest warrants of many victims of the Terror. When Danton and the Indulgents were on trial in April 1794, it was Robespierre who had decided that they should be arrested and signed the warrants. And when it looked as though Danton might be using his revolutionary reputation to defend himself successfully, Robespierre was involved in changing the law. Now anyone who insulted the justice system could be removed from court. This new law was used to remove Danton so that he was no longer able to defend himself and he and the rest of the Indulgents were convicted and guillotined quickly. Their deaths are seen as the start of the Great Terror. He was also responsible for drawing up the murderous Law of Prairial. This widened the definition of anti-revolutionary behaviour to include almost anything.

On the other hand, Robespierre was just one member of the CPS and after his overthrow the surviving members did try to continue the Terror. They were stopped by the deputies in the National Convention. So, both those groups should take some of the responsibility for the Terror. Also, there are a number of factors in Robespierre's defence. He may have called for harsh measures against the federalist revolt in Lyons, but he was shocked by the brutal tactics of some of the representatives on mission, like Collot d'Herbois, and he was trying to move against them. That was one reason why they joined the plot to overthrow him. And while his speeches about conspiracy did raise

> There is some judgement here although this could be more clearly expressed.

> Some clear context applied to the question, albeit some confusion over the starting point of the Terror.

> Good detail and attempts to introduce the other side of the argument signalled in the opening paragraph.

> Good detail but here misses the opportunity to expand on how Prairial speeded up trials and made guilty verdicts far more likely, by abolishing defence counsels and public cross-examination of defendants and witnesses.

the political temperature and did lead to more people becoming victims of the Terror, there was an assassination attempt on his life and he was overthrown by a conspiracy, so he was not entirely wrong there.

It is also important to note that when the revolution looked safe after the defeat of the federal revolts, and when all foreign troops had been driven out of France in early 1794, Robespierre was initially prepared to consider an end to the Terror. He did approve Desmoulins's early newspaper editions and might have supported the Indulgents and their clemency committee, but he couldn't because of the pressure from extremists like the Hébertists and from other members of the CPS.

There is also the argument that the Great Terror was actually all about the policy of centralisation, which the CPS had followed from its early days as necessary to mobilise France to win the war. The Committee sent out the representatives on mission to enforce its policies in the provinces and the armies and, because it didn't trust local courts to convict, had all suspects sent to Paris. This led to overcrowding in the Paris prisons and, as the Committee believed that all of the suspects identified by the police bureau were guilty, that made speeding up the trial procedure the obvious solution. This argument clearly makes the Committee as a whole responsible rather than Robespierre as just one member.

In conclusion, it is clear that Robespierre must take some responsibility for the Terror. He did lead in the Jacobin Club and was very influential in the National Convention and his signature was on the arrest warrants of many of its victims. But he did not act alone. He was one member of the CPS, so they should take part of the responsibility, as should those representatives on mission, like Collot d'Herbois. In the end, it was the deputies of the National Convention who brought the Terror to an end after Robespierre's execution, so it is arguable that they could have stopped it sooner. It was all too convenient for the Thermidorians to blame the Terror on someone who was dead so as to avoid taking their share of the responsibility.

> There is balance as the candidate offers a strong counter-argument here.

> There is clear judgement at the end of this paragraph.

> The conclusion does offer a succinct judgement although it could be made clearer.

While there are on occasions some weaknesses in communication and some of the judgement could be developed more, the answer does offer some substantial analysis and evaluation. There is clear structure to the response that is fully focused upon the question and offers a range of supporting information.

## Reverse engineering

The best essays are based on careful plans. Read the essay and the comments and try to work out the general points of the plan used to write the essay. Once you have done this, note down the specific examples used to support each general point.

Below is a sample Level 5 essay. It was written in response to an A-level question.

'In the years 1793 and 1794 the Committee of Public Safety was forced to follow the policy of Terror.' Assess the validity of this view.

At the start of 1793 the problems facing the Committee of Public Safety (CPS) were huge. The first and most serious was the threat of invasion from the forces of the Third Coalition. This carried with it the threat of the overthrow of the revolution and their own deaths as regicides. Organising the country for war was a massive task. At the same time they faced opposition from others inside France, from federalists and counter-revolutionaries. Finally, they faced arguments from other revolutionaries who disagreed with their solutions to the problems.

> This introduction takes a clear viewpoint from the start and offers a justification based upon the problems the CPS faced.

The committee was set up on 6 April 1793 under the leadership initially of Danton and became essentially a war cabinet. The forces of the Third Coalition countries – Austria, Prussia, Britain, Spain and Sardinia – invaded France and the first task of the Committee of Public Safety was to raise a big enough army to fight them all. This was organised by Carnot. He was behind the levée en masse, the call up of all unmarried men between the ages of 18 and 25 which produced an army of 800,000 men by 1794. Carnot also organised the war economy, with everything directed towards centralised control. The munitions industry was expanded and workers moved to the war effort. Women were involved, too, in hospitals. All this provided France with the armies to win victory. But that was not enough by itself. The generals leading the armies had to be trustworthy. Earlier in the revolution, generals like Lafayette and, later, Dumouriez had tried to turn their armies on the revolution and when that failed they had defected to the enemy, the Austrians, in each case. So it was necessary for the Committee to send representatives on mission to the armies to bolster their morale and to keep an eye on their generals. In 1793 two generals were recalled and guillotined. This terror tactic was necessary when they were fighting an enemy on the outside and within their own ranks.

> The candidate is referring to Generals Custine and Houchard.

> There is detailed knowledge deployed and the key link back to the question is made at the end of the paragraph.

The representatives on mission were a very important part of how the Committee worked, as it tried to ensure that its orders were followed. One of the weaknesses of the Ancien Régime was the regional differences and centralising power was key to the Committee's success. That others might want different policies is illustrated by the arguments over the fate of the king at the start of 1793. The Girondins wanted to keep him alive as a hostage and wanted to give the whole country a vote on his fate. This sort of difference was to lead to the later purge of the Girondins which was part of the Terror.

> Answer reiterates concept of centralisation and tries to introduce another theme – the Girondins – although not very effectively.

One consequence of the levée en masse was the revolt of the Vendée. This rebellion, with its royalist character, was very successful in its early stages, with revolutionary supporters murdered, troops routed and cities captured or sacked. It threatened the survival of the revolution and was capable of putting large armies into action. Any troops sent to fight in the Vendée were troops that could have been fighting the foreign invaders, so the Committee had to be ruthless in suppressing the revolt. In the aftermath of the revolt, reprisals led to the execution of thousands, some deliberately drowned in the River Loire. This in turn sparked guerrilla war and even harsher reprisals, a vicious spiral that led to over 150,000 deaths. It can be argued, though, that the Committee had no alternative to these tactics as the rebels could have combined with a British invasion. There were attempts to link with the British fleet at Granville.

> The answer gets back on track linking to the second paragraph and refers back to the question.

The move towards centralising power also prompted the federal revolts in cities like Lyons, Bordeaux and Marseilles. This revolt began as resentment over the control that the Paris Commune had over the direction of the revolution, but it changed in character to counter-revolution. In Lyon Jacobins were guillotined and in Toulon the British fleet was welcomed. As with the Vendée, the Committee had no alternative but to suppress the revolts as swiftly as they could, but it could be argued that the reprisals that followed need not have been as brutal as they were. The massed shooting with cannons in Lyons was definitely a terror tactic but it is worth remembering that there were disagreements on the Committee about this. Robespierre had argued for a harsh response and Couthon was recalled for not being harsh enough, although later the actions of Collot d'Herbois who ordered the use of cannons were questioned.

The answer begins to offer limited balance here.

Linked with the use of terror to suppress the federalist revolts was the use of terror against other revolutionaries. The Girondins were mixed up with the federalist revolts, in part as the causes and in part as participants, and they were arrested, convicted and guillotined. When it looked as though they might be acquitted, changes were made to the laws to ensure their trial was cut short. Did the Committee have any choice in this matter? If the Girondins had won the power struggle would they not have sent the Committee members to the guillotine? Certainly they had advocated violence when arguing for war back in 1792. Plus, there was another group putting pressure on the Committee – extremists like the Hébertists, backed by sans-culotte power, who wanted more Terror. It was only after the war against the Third Coalition had been won that the Committee were able to move against the sans-culottes by limiting their power to organise in the Paris Commune in September 1793 and then by taking control of local government in December 1793. In 1794 the Committee than moved on to destroy the Hébertists.

The candidate explores some of the uncertainty in the question here.

However, the final stage of the Terror in 1794 is more difficult to explain. The Committee passed the law on General Police and the Law of Prairial, which allowed the Great Terror to happen. Perhaps the biggest problem for the members of the Committee then was how to stop the Terror without themselves becoming its victims. There had been assassinations and attempted assassinations – and it is worth remembering, too, that after they toppled Robespierre, the surviving members of the Committee tried to carry on the Terror. That was stopped by the National Convention itself – several of them ended up either guillotined or condemned to the dry guillotine of exile in Guiana.

In conclusion, the Committee's freedom of action was severely limited by the threat of foreign war and by internal rebellions in 1793. They had to take strong action to preserve both the revolution and themselves. It can be argued that after the war was won and the san-culottes controlled, they might have managed to bring an end to the Terror sooner, but in the atmosphere of conspiracy and plots, and with the real threat of assassination, it is understandable that they responded as they did.

**The response is consistently analytical. It is well supported with precise evidence and offers balance while considering the question. It has a clear structure, is controlled and well written for the most part and has a reasonable conclusion.**

**Sustaining an argument**

The sign of a strong Level 5 answer is the way it sustains an argument from start to finish, with each paragraph developing a key part of the argument. Examine the opening and closing paragraphs carefully and highlight where the candidate has presented and concluded their argument. In addition, give a heading to each paragraph to indicate what part of the argument is being developed.

# 4 The Directory and Napoleon's rise to power, 1795–99

## The aftermath of the Terror

### The Thermidorian reaction

The Thermidorians were the men who overthrew Robespierre. They included the surviving members of the CPS and the CGS, ex-Terrorists, and the deputies of the National Convention. Robespierre and his associates were labelled as **Terrorists** and blamed for the Terror. Some who had not died with him at Thermidor were also guillotined.

The deputies of the National Convention moved to end the Terror and reverse the process of centralisation by:
- ensuring that the membership of the CPS and CGS was changed frequently
- setting up new committees to share government responsibilities
- reorganising the Revolutionary Tribunal
- repealing the law of Prairial
- releasing all suspects from prison
- abolishing the Paris Commune
- closing the Jacobin Club.

It also established freedom of worship for all religion.

### The White Terror

In Paris gangs of young men, **Gilded Youth**, intimidated and beat up former Jacobins, militants and sans-culottes. They stoned the Jacobin Club, which was used as a pretext for its closure.

In the provinces the violence was worse. In the south in Lyon and the Rhone valley, the Terror had been so brutal there were savage reprisals against ex-Terrorists. Prison massacres and street murders cost as many as 2,000 lives in 1795. The government was unable or unwilling to stop this violence continuing into 1796.

In the west guerrilla warfare flared again in the Vendée with the **Chouan** movement. This was a response to the brutal suppression of 1793, in opposition to conscription, and had royalist links. With British assistance, an émigré army landed in Brittany, but this was defeated and hundreds executed. The violence was suppressed by 1796 by the deployment of a massive army.

### The 1795 Parisian risings

The Thermidorians abolished price controls in 1794. This led to a fall in the value of the assignat and high inflation. At the same time a harsh winter led to food shortages.

#### Germinal 1 April

The shortages led to a huge demonstration in Paris. Demonstrators calling for bread and the release of former members of the CPS surrounded the National Convention. However, they gained no support from among the deputies and when the National Guard stayed loyal to the Convention they dispersed. In the aftermath some ex-Terrorists were exiled to the **'dry guillotine'** of Guiana.

#### Prairial 20–22 May

This journée was more serious, as some demonstrators were armed and some National Guards joined them. To begin with, the National Convention deputies were forced at cannon point to give in, but when loyal army units arrived they were able to regain control. Some of the demonstration leaders were arrested, tried and executed, others imprisoned. Thousands were disarmed and the power of the sans-culottes was finally broken. The loyalty of the army to the government was crucial, something that had been missing in 1789.

## Identify the tone and emphasis of a source

Study the source below. Don't focus on the content – instead, focus on the:

- language
- sentence structure
- emphasis of the source
- overall tone.

What does the tone and emphasis of the source suggest about its value, in terms of the:

- reliability of the evidence?
- utility of the evidence for studying the Thermidorian reaction?

Note: Stanislas Fréron had been threatened by Robespierre before Thermidor and, as well as sitting in the Convention, organised the Gilded Youth.

### SOURCE A

An extract from the memoires *Souvenirs thermidoriens* (1844) of Georges Duval, a playwright who lived in Paris during the Revolution.

Fréron's Gilded Youth, which was not in the least gilded, were called that because of their tone, their manners and the cleanliness of their dress which was in marked contrast with the language, the vulgar manners, and the official filthiness of the Jacobin costume. It was made up of all the young people who belonged to the upper classes of Paris society which had more or less suffered from the Revolution, several of whom had relatives or friends who had been drowned in that enormous shipwreck [that is, the Terror]. It was also made up of all the clerks of notaries, solicitors or appraisers, almost all the merchants' clerks, and finally all those who belonged to the honourable bourgeoisie. United, they formed in the middle of Paris a large enough army for the Convention to count on to oppose, if the occasion arose, the Jacobin masses who, in spite of the defeat of their leaders, were still solid and threatening.

## Support or challenge?

Below is a sample exam question which asks you to assess the validity of a specific statement. Below this are some general statements that are relevant to the question. Using your own knowledge and the information on the opposite page, decide whether these statements support or challenge the statement in the question.

'The Thermidorians were successful in bringing an end to the violence of the Terror in the years 1794–95.' Assess the validity of this view.

| | Support | Challenge |
|---|---|---|
| The Revolutionary Tribunal was abolished | | |
| White Terror | | |
| Law of Prairial repealed | | |
| The Jacobin Club was closed after the attack by the Gilded Youth | | |
| The Paris Commune was abolished | | |
| Membership of committees was changed more frequently | | |
| Paris uprisings in 1795 | | |

# The establishment of the Directory, part 1

## The constitution

The Thermidorians produced a new constitution in 1795. It was designed to prevent a return to a monarchy, to a dictatorship like that of the CPS and to control by the common people, the sans-culottes.

The National Convention (legislature) was replaced by two councils:

| Council of Five Hundred | Council of Ancients |
| --- | --- |
| All members had to be over 30 | All 250 members had to be over 40 |
| Initiated legislation | Approved or rejected legislation. |

Annual elections for both changed one-third of members each year. All males over 21 who paid direct taxes (around 5.5 million men) could vote for electors. The electors, rich men who paid high taxes (around 30,000 men), voted for Council members.

The CPS (executive) was replaced by the Directory of Five, who were:
- chosen by the Ancients from a list drawn up by the Five Hundred
- in office for five years
- chosen one at a time by lot to retire each year.

### Weaknesses of the constitution

- Yearly elections led to instability.
- There was no mechanism to resolve disputes between the Directors and the two Councils. This could, and did, lead to stalemate and inaction.

## Economic and financial problems and policies

### Economic problems

The Directory first tried to solve the problem of inflation by issuing a new paper currency. When that failed and had to be withdrawn, metal coins became the legal currency. As there were not enough coins in circulation, trade and commerce was hindered. **Deflation** was the result. This failure made the Directory unpopular with all sections of society.

### Financial problems

The Directory was more successful in solving the problem of government finances. In September 1797 two-thirds of the national debt was written off through the issue of bonds to government creditors. These bonds could be used to buy national property – property confiscated from the Crown, the Church and others. However, these bonds fell in value until they became worthless. This was known at the time as the 'bankruptcy of two-thirds'. The debt was now gone, but at the cost of the Directory losing the support of all those original government creditors.

For government income, the Directory relied in part on the profits of war – plunder taken from captured territories in Germany and Italy. This allowed the Directory to function, but at the cost of greater reliance on the army and on an aggressive war policy.

The lasting solution was provided by finance minister Vincent Ramel. In 1798 he reformed the tax system by:
- introducing four new direct taxes – the tax on windows and doors hit the rich hardest
- reintroducing an indirect tax, the octrois, a tax on goods entering towns
- making tax collection more efficient.

The effect of these policies was to balance government finances, but at the cost of alienating those sections of society adversely affected by the bankruptcy and new taxes.

# Judgements on the value of a source

**a**

Read Source A below and the alternative answers that reflect on its provenance.

Which answer will gain the higher level in the mark scheme, and why?

> The source is valuable to a historian investigating the problems faced by the Directory, because it reflects the opinion of a Director who would have been very well placed to understand the difficulties the government faced.

> The source is partially valuable to a historian investigating the problems faced by the Directory, because it reflects the view of a Director who was well placed to understand the difficulties it faced. We do need to remember, however, that he was forced to resign. It is less useful for revealing the views of those in the legislative councils.

Having made your choice, read Source B and write an answer which mirrors the answer above that you have chosen as your model.

## SOURCE A

From the memoires of a Louis-Marie Larévellière-Lépaux, who served as a Director from November 1795 to June 1799, when he was forced to resign in the Coup of Prairial. Here he reflects on the constitution that established the Directory.

Its short duration was principally due to the circumstances that attended its birth … and prevented it from being perfected. Before it could achieve a certain degree of stability, which time alone can confer on political institutions, it was assailed with the utmost violence by factions at home and intrigues abroad. Europe in arms leagued against it and all means of governing in the midst of this fearful tempest still had to be created. To this, admittedly, must be added vices which should have been corrected. The executive power was too weak and it had no legal means of defending itself. … To defend the constitution and to defend themselves, the Directors had to employ force, as on 18 fructidor, and in the process the constitution was violated and lost the greater part of its own force.

## SOURCE B

From the memoires of Madame de Staël, daughter of Jacques Necker. She was in exile during the Revolution but returned after Thermidor and supported the Directory. Here she reflects on its early achievements.

One has to give credit to the Directory. The first 20 months which succeeded the establishment of the Republic constitute a particularly remarkable period of administration. Five men chosen in anger, came to power in the most unfavourable circumstances. … Paper money was reduced to almost a thousandth of its nominal value; there was not as much as 100,000 francs in cash in the treasury; food supplies were so scarce that the discontent of the people was barely contained; the insurrection in the Vendée was still going on; civil unrest had given rise to bands of brigands, who committed horrible excesses in the countryside; finally, almost all the French armies were disorganised.

In six months, the Directory raised France from this deplorable situation. Coin smoothly replaced paper money; old proprietors lived in peace next to those who had acquired national goods; roads in the countryside had become perfectly safe; the army was very successful; the liberty of the press made a come-back; elections followed their legal course, and one would have been able to say that France was free, if the two classes of nobles and priests had enjoyed the same guarantees as other citizens.

# The establishment of the Directory, part 2

## Political problems and policies

France was divided not just by a desire for revenge but also by deep political differences. On the left were the **neo-Jacobins**, who remained a force even after the White Terror and the closure of the Jacobins Club. On the right were the Royalists, who were released from prison or had returned from exile. The Directory needed to draw upon each side at times to survive.

## Vendémiaire Uprising, October 1795

The royalists were split. Some wanted a return to constitutional monarchy under the imprisoned Dauphin. When he died in 1795, his uncle, the Comte de Provence, issued the Verona Declaration, promising to restore the ancient constitution and to return all lands to their original owners. In this political climate the National Convention deputies passed the law of two-thirds to ensure that the new councils would be dominated by those committed to continuing the revolution.

This prompted the Vendémiaire Uprising. Up to 25,000 demonstrators surrounded the National Convention, but they were dispersed by the army using cannon (Napoleon's 'whiff of grapeshot'). While over 300 died in the fighting there was little repression afterwards, but the National Guard was placed under the command of the General of the Army of the Interior, **Napoleon**.

## Conspiracy of Equals, March 1796

Babeuf planned a revolutionary uprising, using the police and army to set up a dictatorship. This would then create a very different French society, one organised on lines very close to communism. He was betrayed, arrested, tried and executed.

## Brotier Plot, January 1797

Brotier, a royalist agent, and his fellow conspirators were arrested for planning to persuade the troops in Paris to overthrow the government.

## Coup of Fructidor, September 1797

In 1797 the royalists did well in the elections and were close to gaining control of the Councils. Two of the Directors were sympathetic, too. The remaining Directors called upon the army for support. Troops surrounded the Council chambers and many royalists were arrested including two Directors and 27 Deputies. Then, 65 were deported to Guiana. Thereafter the election results were overturned. The Directors were in control of the Councils and in effect the constitution had been overthrown.

In the aftermath, émigrés were given two weeks to leave France and clergy were forced to swear an oath rejecting any support for royalty.

## Coup of Floréal, May 1798

In 1798 the neo-Jacobins did well in the elections, although they were nowhere near controlling the Councils. Even so, the Directors made sure that the elections of 127 deputies were annulled and then chose their replacements.

## Strengths and weaknesses of the Directory

| Strengths | Weaknesses |
| --- | --- |
| Solved government finances | The Constitution itself |
| Had the support of the army | Deep divisions in French society |
| Destroyed sans-culotte power | Reliance on war and hence the army |
|  | Undemocratic actions – for example, Floreal |

## Simple essay style

Below is a sample exam question. Use your own knowledge and the information on the opposite page to produce a plan for this question. Choose four general points and provide three pieces of specific information to support each general point.

Once you have planned your essay, write the introduction and conclusion for the essay. The introduction should list the points to be discussed in the essay. The conclusion should summarise the key points and justify which point was the most important.

> The major achievement of the Directory was that it provided democratic government for four years. Assess the validity of this view.

## Identify the tone and emphasis of a source

Study the source below. Don't focus on the content, instead focus on the:
- language
- sentence structure
- emphasis of the source
- overall tone.

What does the tone and emphasis of the source suggest about its value, in terms of the:
- reliability of the evidence
- utility of the evidence for studying the Directory?

### SOURCE A

From a letter by Nicolas Ruault, a Parisian bookseller, to his brother. Here he is commenting upon the situation in the city in the year III.

Paris, 24 Germinal, Year III

Public affairs are a thousand times worse in Paris than with you, my dear friend; we are lost here in an immense chasm; we have become a hydra with 650,000 heads with as many empty stomachs that have been hungry now for a long time, and it is impossible, not necessarily to satisfy the hunger, but to half feed it. I dare not tell you all that is said, all the curses one hears in the long queues which form every evening, every night, at the bakers' doors, in the hope of getting, after five or six hours' wait, sometimes half a pound of biscuit per person, sometimes half a pound of bad bread, sometimes 6 ounces of rice or 6 ounces of biscuit per person. And yet the government treats the 4 or 5,000 men who lose half their working day waiting for this minuscule portion of wretched food, who complain about their poverty and the horror of their existence, as seditious. It has long been known that hunger is seditious by nature; ... Banish that, and these supposedly seditious people will disappear. They will not break into the august French Senate again, as they did on the 12th of this month (April), to cry, 'Give us bread! Give us bread!'

# Military campaigns and expansion abroad

REVISED

When the Directory came to power there were no foreign armies on French soil. By 1796 France only faced Britain and Austria. The other countries of the First Coalition had been knocked out of the war and two of them, Spain and Holland, had become French allies.

An aggressive war policy was followed. The plunder helped finance the government and war kept ambitious generals occupied. Also some Directors, it was alleged, had corrupt links with war profiteers and so directly benefited themselves.

## Napoleon's background, character and military leadership

Napoleon was born in Corsica in 1769, one year after it joined France. The son of a minor aristocratic family, he was sent to France for his education. He entered the École Militaire in Paris in 1784 and was its first Corsican graduate. If it had not been for the Revolution he might have had a modest career. However, after 1789 he was able to take advantage of the increased opportunities for able officers. Originally a Corsican patriot, he became a supporter of the revolution. His pro-revolutionary pamphlet brought him to the attention of Robespierre's younger brother, Augustin, a useful connection.

To some historians, he exhibited two aspects of the Corsican stereotype. One, putting family first, hence his later appointment of his brothers to kingships. Two, seeking revenge, such as the judicial murder of the Duc d'Enghien and the savage reprisals against civilian resistance in Palestine, Italy and Spain.

## Napoleon's contribution to French success

At the siege of Toulon, as commander of the artillery, he devised the plan which drove the British navy out. This won him promotion to brigadier general in charge of the artillery of the army of Italy. After Thermidor, his association with Robespierre led to a brief spell in prison, but being out of Paris saved him from a worse fate. A number of military commands followed, but his career seemed blocked when he refused to serve against the Vendéan rebels. However, in 1795 he was again in the right place at the right time – Paris. Placed in charge of the temporary forces assembled to defend the National Convention against the Vendémiaire uprising, his use of cannon fire was crucial. This earned him command of the army of Italy.

## Italian campaign, 1796–97

Napoleon fought an unexpectedly successful campaign in Italy. He took over a small army and, with his charismatic leadership, won a series of victories. In the process, he collected a lot of money which helped finance the Directory. He also sent back troops to help the Directory in the coup of Fructidor. After driving the Austrians out of Italy his advance into Austria forced them to sue for peace. Napoleon negotiated the advantageous Treaty of Campo Formio in October 1797, without consulting the Directory, and returned to France a hero.

## Egypt, 1798

After Italy, Napoleon sailed to Egypt to attack British interests. His army won the Battle of the Pyramids but was unsuccessful in capturing Syria. Meanwhile, his fleet was destroyed by Nelson at the Battle of the Nile, leaving his army trapped. In August he received news that took him back to France. His abandoned army remained in Egypt until 1801, when it was defeated by a British army.

**Whole A-level question**

Read the three sources and the question. Write notes assessing the value of each source, using headings such as 'content and knowledge', 'provenance' and 'tone'.

With reference to these sources and your understanding of the historical context, assess the value of these three sources to an historian studying the importance of war to the Directory.

## SOURCE A

Adapted from Napoleon's Proclamation to the Army of Italy, 26 April 1796.

Friends, I promise you this conquest, but there is one condition you have to swear to fulfil, and that is to respect the people you deliver, and to suppress the horrible pillage to which scoundrels encouraged by our enemies deliver themselves. Without it, you will not be the liberators of the people, you will be their scourge. ... Your victories, your courage, your success, the blood of our brothers who died in battle, all will be lost, even honour and glory. As for me and the generals who have your confidence, we would be ashamed to command an army without discipline, without bridle, which knows no other law than force. But, invested with the national authority, strengthened by justice and the law, I will know how to impose respect for the laws of humanity and honour which that little group of men without courage and without hearts trample underfoot. ... I will ensure that the rules I have passed are strictly observed. Looters will be shot without pity; several have been already. I have had occasion to note with pleasure the zeal with which good soldiers have executed these orders.

## SOURCE B

Adapted from a letter from Napoleon to the Directory in Paris.

Headquarters, Pistoia, 26 June 1796

I enclose the terms of the armistice with the Pope. M d'Azara, the actual negotiator, had the impudence to offer us 5 millions in cash and 3 in kind. I stood out for 40 millions, including 10 in kind. Seeing that I would not come down, he went to the Government Commissioners, and managed to worm out of them our weak point, namely our inability to march on Rome. After that I could only get 20 millions out of him, in spite of a night march on Ravenna. I had made it a condition all along that he should hand over the treasures of Our Lady of Loretto, and I thought he had agreed to it: ...

## SOURCE C

Extracts from the treaty signed between France and the Cisalpine Republic, 21 February 1798.

The French Republic recognises the Cisalpine Republic as a free and independent power; it guarantees its liberty, its independence, and the abolition of every government before the one that now administers it.

The Cisalpine Republic having requested the French Republic for an army corps sufficient to maintain its liberty, its independence, and its internal peace, as well as to preserve it fro all aggression on the part of its neighbours, the two republics have agreed upon the following articles in connection.

Until otherwise agreed thereon, there shall be in the Cisalpine Republic a body of French troops amounting to 25,000 men, including the staff and administration. The said body shall be composed of 22,000 infantry, 2,500 cavalry, and 500 artillery, either horse or of the line.

The Cisalpine Republic will furnish annually to the French Republic, for payment and maintenance of the said troops, a sum of 18,000,000 which shall be paid, in 12 equal monthly instalments, into the funds of the army, and in the case of war, the necessary supplement of supplies.

# The coup of Brumaire and the establishment of the Consulate, part 1

## The decline in power and popularity of the Directory

A number of events, decisions and developments in 1798 and 1799 contributed to this decline.

### Jourdan's Law, September 1798

Conscription was reintroduced to rebuild the size of the army. This provoked widespread resistance.

### The Second Coalition

Encouraged by British success, the Second Coalition formed in 1799. As the Revolutionary War continued, the French armies were pushed back into France from Germany and Italy. This meant the Directory could not continue to be funded by plunder. Also, the threat of invasion made it unpopular. France was weary of war.

### Coup of Prairial, June 1799

With the war going badly and the Directors getting the blame, the neo-Jacobin-led Councils felt strong enough to purge two of the Directors. This was followed by two new laws. The first was a forced loan on the rich, which was hated and resisted.

### The Law of Hostages

The second law was the Law of Hostages. Any area seen as resisting the government could be declared 'disturbed' and then the local authorities could arrest relatives of nobles, émigrés and rebels, imprison them and confiscate their property. This law was never applied, but the strength of the neo-Jacobins raised fears of a return to Terror.

All these problems led to a breakdown in government in parts of France.

## The Coup of Brumaire

In late 1799 the military situation improved as the partners in the Second Coalition failed to co-operate and were separately defeated. **Sieyès**, now a Director, plotted a coup. He wanted to restore the power of the executive and knew a democratic approach was impossible due to the strength of the neo-Jacobins in the Councils. He needed the support of the army and of a General – his eventual choice was Napoleon, recently returned from Egypt. Once again, Napoleon was in the right place at the right time.

Sieyès planned to move the Councils out of Paris to Saint Cloud and did so on 10 November 1799, on the pretext of a neo-Jacobin plot. Once in Saint Cloud, Napoleon was persuaded to address the Councils, who had come to realise who the plotters really were. In the Council of Five Hundred, Napoleon was attacked by deputies but his soldiers, alerted by his brother, came to his rescue. The Councils were cleared by military force and the plotters issued a decree abolishing the Directory. It had lost so much popularity and legitimacy through its undemocratic actions that no one came forward to defend it.

In its place France was to be ruled by a provisional executive committee of three: Sieyès, Roger Ducos and Napoleon. Sieyès saw Napoleon as providing a figurehead for this new regime, but Napoleon had different ideas. When the three consuls met that evening, Napoleon insisted that he should become First Consul, the head of state with complete control and, as he controlled the army, that is how the argument ended.

## RAG – rate the timeline

Below are a sample exam question and a timeline. Read the question, study the timeline and, using three coloured pens, put a red, amber or green star next to the events to show:

- red: events and policies that have no relevance to the question
- amber: events and policies that have some significance to the question
- green: events and policies that are directly relevant to the question.

To what extent was Napoleon's seizure of power at Brumaire the consequence of the weaknesses of the government of the Directory?

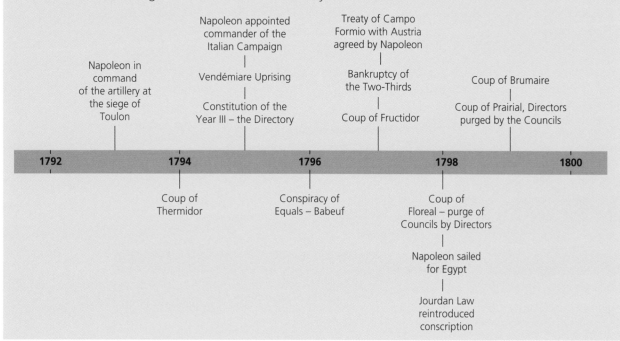

## Recommended reading

Below is a list of suggested further reading on the Directory.

- Dave Martin, *The French Revolution*, pages 114–122 (2015)
- Peter Jones, *The French Revolution*, *second edition*, pages 77–91 (2010)
- William Doyle, *The Oxford History of the French Revolution*, *second edition*, pages 318–340 (2012)

# The coup of Brumaire and the establishment of the Consulate, part 2

## The constitution

The new constitution was the result of six weeks of negotiations between Sieyès, Roger Ducos and Napoleon. Napoleon was to be First Consul with complete executive power in war and peace. The other two Consuls had an advisory function only.

The Senate was intended by Sieyès to act as a balance to the power of the executive. He even appointed half its members who then chose the rest. It was a well-paid and prestigious position. Appointment was for life and it grew in size with new senators nominated by Napoleon. Instead of challenging him, its members became keen to agree with the man who provided them with gifts of money and land.

There was no property qualification for voters. All men over 21 were eligible to vote, but there were no elections. Instead, at each stage there were presentations of candidates suitable for appointment – it was not democratic.

The male population (around 6,000,000) chose the Communal List (600,000) who chose the Department List (60,000) who chose the National List, the Notables (6,000).

### The Notables

This was the key group. The Notables were the highest-taxed men, the richest, in each department. They were to be replaced every three years. From their number the Senate chose the (legislative bodies) who were to serve for five years:

| Tribunate | Legislature |
| --- | --- |
| 100 members aged over 25 | 300 members aged over 30 |
| Discussed legislation drafted by the Senate but was not able to vote on it | Voted on legislation in secret but was not able to discuss it |

The executive was made up of the First Consul, Senate and Council of State.

| The First Consul | Senate | Council of State |
| --- | --- | --- |
| Appointed all ministers and initiated all legislation | 60 members aged over 40 | 30–40 members chosen by the First Consul |
| | Appointed for life | |
| Along with the other two Consuls, he was elected for 10 years | Nominated by the First Consul | Nominated all central and local officials |
| | | Helped initiate legislation |
| | Verified legislation | |

## Strengths and weaknesses

The new constitution avoided the instability of annual elections and the potential for stalemate of the previous constitution. Instead of the system of checks and balances it centralised power in the hands of the First Consul. This left the way open to Napoleon's military dictatorship, as he had the backing of the army. It was drawn up in a short period but put into action illegally, before the **plebiscite** to approve it could be organised. It was endorsed by the plebiscite in 1800.

## Napoleon's position and the state of France by 1799

By the end of 1799 the tide of the Revolutionary War had turned. France was victorious, internal royalist revolts had been suppressed and Napoleon was popular. He offered strong government, which was what the propertied classes wanted. The Directory had appeared unable to protect them from the twin threats of monarchists and neo-Jacobins. While there was some public apathy regarding political affairs, the key point was that Napoleon had the support of the army.

**Delete as applicable**    a

Below are a sample exam question and a paragraph written in answer to this question. Read the paragraph and decide which of the possible options (in bold) is most appropriate. Delete the least appropriate options and complete the paragraph by justifying your selection.

'By the end of 1799 Napoleon's position as First Consul of France was completely secure.' Assess the validity of this view.

By the end of 1799 Napoleon's position as First Consul of France was secure to a **great/ fair/limited extent**. For example, the Revolutionary War had turned in France's favour. The royalist revolts had been suppressed and Napoleon was popular. He offered strong government which was what the propertied classes wanted. At the same time the new constitution avoided the instability of annual elections and the potential for stalemate of the previous constitution. However, it was illegally put into action before the plebiscite to approve it had been organised. This presented an **extremely/moderately/slightly difficult** problem for Napoleon because

_____

_____

 **Identify relevant content**

Read the following source and the question. Go through the source and highlight the sections that are relevant for the focus of the question and annotate in the margin the main points.

Assess the value of this source for the historian studying the condition of France at Brumaire in 1799.

### SOURCE A

From a letter by Napoleon replying to Baron de Beytz, a Belgian who he believed opposed his rise to power, written in Paris 24 November 1799.

I want you to rally the mass of the people. The simple title of French citizen is worth far more than that of Royalist, Clichien, Jacobin, Feuillant, or any of those thousand-and-one denominations which have sprung, during the past ten years, from the spirit of faction, and which are hurling the nation into an abyss from which the time has at last come to rescue it, once and for all.

That is the aim of all my efforts. It is that upon which is centred, from this moment, the regard of all thoughtful men, the esteem of the people, and the hope of glory.

# Exam focus

Below is a sample Level 5 answer. It was written in response to an A-level question.

'The Directory was a successful government up to the point where it was overthrown by the coup of Brumaire.' Assess the validity of this view.

The Directory was a successful government for the first two years. It resisted the internal threats from royalists on the right and neo-Jacobins on the left, while solving some of France's financial problems. It also fought a successful war against the forces of the First Coalition. However, it was less successful from 1797 onwards and when it was overthrown by Napoleon in the coup of Brumaire it had few defenders left.

> Good introduction giving a judgement qualified in terms of time.

If the Thermidorians brought the Terror to an end, they did not succeed in ending the bitter political divisions which the Directory was left to deal with. They were unable to rely on sans-culotte power to maintain their position. Instead they had to rely upon the army and this did have its problems. When the regime was threatened by a royalist uprising at Vendémiaire in October 1795 it was the army, led by Napoleon with his use of cannons, that saved the day. And again, later, when the Directors were threatened by the election of so many neo-Jacobin deputies, it was again the army that they relied upon to enforce their actions. Having army support was a strength, but also a weakness if it was taken away. This led the Directory into fighting wars to keep ambitious generals occupied, such as Napoleon's Egyptian campaign which sparked off the formation of the Second Coalition.

> The answer takes a thematic rather than a chronological approach that reinforces its analytical nature.

The political divisions were deeply rooted in the violence of the years of Terror, and after Thermidor the White Terror was a backlash against the Jacobins. The Directory never entirely controlled this violence. When local juries failed to convict those responsible the Directory tried dividing France into military districts and set up military commissions to judge cases and employed generals to maintain law and order. This never entirely worked and its undemocratic nature served to help erode the democratic foundations that the Directory rested on.

> A nuanced approach.

In terms of political plots, it was more successful. Gracchus Babeuf's Conspiracy of Equals plot in 1796 was detected and nipped in the bud, as was that of the royalist, André Brotier. Meanwhile, the émigré landings, with British assistance, at Quiberon Bay and on the Ile de Yeu off the coast of the Vendée, were also successfully defeated.

> Succinct and supported point made.

Abroad, the Directory was successful in defeating the First Coalition, especially thanks to Napoleon's victories in Italy. The benefits of this were the plunder and payments extorted from the defeated enemies, the new territories of Nice and Savoy that were annexed and the creation of satellite republics – Cisalpine and Ligurian. These were a source of income and men for France's armies. This new income went towards solving the problem of government finance, something that can be traced through the revolutionary years back to Louis XVI's Ancien Régime. This was only a short-term solution, however, unless France was to remain constantly at war.

> Again, the case for success is balanced with its flaws.

In February 1797 the paper currency, the assignat, had to be withdrawn because it had plummeted in value. Symptomatic of that was the fact that the Directors themselves received their salaries in grain, not assignats. Their efforts to reform the paper currency failed and in 1787 metal coins were the only currency – and as there was a shortage of coinage this hampered economic activity. Longer term, the Directory came up with two solutions. The first was writing off two-thirds of the national debt by issuing government bonds. These could be used to buy lands confiscated from the Church and the nobility. However, they fell in value too – this became known as the bankruptcy of two-thirds. It reduced the national debt and interest payments on it, but at the price of alienating all those who had lost out – so it was a success in one respect but a failure in terms of keeping support.

**Good use of supporting information.**

The second solution was provided by the Finance Minister, Vincent Ramel. He reformed the tax system and introduced new direct taxes, such as one on windows, and reintroduced an indirect tax from the Ancien Régime, the tax on goods taken into towns. He also made tax collection more efficient. This helped finance the Directory but also made it unpopular with both the rich hit by window taxes and by everyone affected by the tax on goods. So, again, success mixed with failure.

**When looking at the economy the candidate could have mentioned the successful introduction of the metric system.**

If these measures lost the Directory some support, it was their methods of dealing with political opponents in September 1797 that represent one of their biggest failures. When the royalists did very well in the annual elections the Directors used the army to help them, in what became known as the coup of Fructidor. Soldiers were used to take control of Paris and 53 deputies and two Directors were arrested. Further elections were cancelled and those arrested were sent to the 'dry guillotine' of Guiana. The Directory had managed to stay in power, but only at the price of undermining its own democratic foundation. This marked the start of its failure.

**A particularly strong paragraph offering a precise judgement.**

The final failure of the Directory was the way in which corruption was allowed to develop, especially in relation to the supply of the army, which was undertaken by private contractors, some of whom amassed vast fortunes through their friendships with Directors. All of this meant that the Directory lost support just when things began to go badly wrong. As already noted, Napoleon's campaign sparked the formation of the Second Coalition and when the war began to go badly the Jourdan Law of September 1798 tried to reintroduce conscription. Just as before, this sparked revolt in some areas like the Vendée, and law and order broke down in other places. As the Directory lost effective control, the ground was fertile for those plotting to overthrow it – and this is what Sieyès did in preparing Brumaire.

**Helpful links made across the essay.**

So, the Directory was a partial success. It was the longest-lasting democratic revolutionary regime and it did provide a measure of law and order at home and victory abroad, up to 1797. It was always hampered by the weaknesses in the constitution on which it was based – this partly explains why the Directors, in the end, resorted to undemocratic methods that undermined their credibility, to the extent that when they were losing control no one came forward to help them. Overall, therefore, I would judge the Directory to have failed to provide a long-term solution to France's search for stable government.

**Clear judgement reached in relation to the question.**

This is a well-structured response which demonstrates good analysis and supported judgement. While there are some imperfections in linking the material to the question, the response takes into account the complexity of trying to reach an overall judgement over the four years of the Directory's existence.

### Sustaining an argument

The sign of a strong Level 5 answer is the way it sustains an argument from start to finish, with each paragraph developing a key part of the argument. Examine the opening and closing paragraphs carefully and highlight where the candidate has presented and concluded the argument. In addition, give a heading to each paragraph to indicate what part of the argument is being developed.

## Political change

### Napoleon's consolidation of power

In February 1800 Napoleon changed how the 83 departments of France were administered. At their head were **prefects**, who had wide powers and responsibilities, including appointing those officials who served under them. As they were appointed and replaced by the First Consul they were agents of central government. The First Consul also appointed the mayors in major towns and nominated the members of the various councils that existed at department and municipal levels. So, as First Consul Napoleon exercised highly centralised control of the administration of France, as well as considerable powers of patronage.

### Life Consul

In December 1800 an assassination attempt on Napoleon failed. Although it was planned by royalists, Napoleon used it as the pretext to deal with neo-Jacobins too – 100 neo-Jacobins were deported. The plot also highlighted how dependent the regime was on Napoleon, which led the Senate to offer Napoleon the Consulship for life. He accepted, if the people agreed – in the plebiscite that followed, over 3,500,000 voted for the motion, with just over 8,000 against. As with each of the plebiscites held, there are debates about how accurate the figures are. Historians agree that there was vote rigging and misreporting. Nevertheless, Napoleon became Life Consul.

At the same time, the Senate was enlarged and the Legislature had more of Napoleon's supporters appointed, giving him greater control of both. Meanwhile, the Tribunate was purged in 1802 for opposing the Civil Code.

### Foreign affairs

Two events made Napoleon's position more secure. The first was the Concordat with the Pope in 1801. This removed the conflict for Catholics between their religion and the state. The second was the Treaty of Amiens (1802), which ended the Revolutionary Wars. This was very popular in France.

### Establishment of Emperor status

Napoleon moved into the Tuileries Palace and began to develop a court life complete with ceremonies and etiquette. Émigrés were allowed to return, the **Legion of Honour** introduced and there were rumours that the nobility would be reintroduced.

In 1804 a plot was uncovered to murder Napoleon and replace him with the Duc d'Enghien, a member of the Bourbon royal family, who was waiting over the border in Baden. The Duc was kidnapped, tried for conspiracy and shot in what some saw as a judicial murder. The property-owning classes feared the reintroduction of the monarchy, with its threat of returning all land to its original owners, and so supported the formal proposal of the Senate that Napoleon be made hereditary Emperor of France. A third plebiscite confirmed that the people agreed. Although the turnout was lower than in previous plebiscites this still showed that Napoleon had support. On 2 December 1804 Napoleon crowned himself Emperor in Paris, in the presence of the Pope, and then crowned his wife, Josephine.

### Constitutional developments

Following Napoleon's coronation the Tribunate and Legislature were rarely consulted. The latter was formally abolished in 1808, while the former only survived by not challenging Napoleon's wishes. Government was conducted through the Senate and the Council of State, both firmly under Napoleon's control.

## Recommended reading

Below is a list of suggested further reading on Napoleon's rise 1799–1804.

- Malcolm Crook, *Napoleon Comes to Power*, pages 71–95 (1998)
- Peter Jones, *The French Revolution*, *second edition*, pages 92–104 (2010)
- Steven Englund, *Napoleon: A political life*, pages 209–237 (2004)

## Introducing and concluding an argument

Look at the key points of the answer.

- How good is the proposed introduction?
- How effective is the proposed conclusion?
- Could either be improved – especially in relation to Level 5 answers?

How accurate is it to say that the Concordat with the Pope was a more important agreement than the Treaty of Amiens for Napoleon as he strengthened his grip on power in France?

**Key points:**

- Treaty of Amiens, 1802, brought peace to a war-weary France.
- The treaty was more of a pause than an end, as fighting broke out again in 1803.
- The Concordat, 1801, removed the problem of divided loyalties – between the revolution and religion.
- The Concordat confirmed that Church lands would not be claimed back.

**Introduction:**

The Treaty of Amiens was an important agreement. It brought the Revolutionary Wars to an end, which was very popular in France. However, the Concordat agreed with the Pope proved to be a more important agreement in the longer term. The Civil Constitution of the Clergy forced many Frenchmen to choose between their religion and the revolution, which was a lasting problem for the revolutionary leaders. Through his Concordat Napoleon was able to bring this conflict of loyalties to an end. Plus, it brought him other benefits.

**Conclusion:**

In conclusion, the Concordat was much more important than the Treaty of Amiens.

# Social change

## Class distinctions and titles

During his reign Napoleon worked to create a body of men who were loyal to him, especially soldiers. He was also effective in winning over many politicians who had initially opposed Brumaire. He did this through gifts, honours, titles and lands.

1 The Legion of Honour was created in 1802. Recipients received a medal which it was fashionable to wear plus an annual sum, quite small for most, but higher for the highest ranks of the order. There were 38,000 members, mostly soldiers, by 1814.

2 Between 1804 and 1808 new titles were created for the leading officials of the new imperial court. Again, there were differing ranks. Some came with lands. Initially these were given to members of Napoleon's family but later to his leading generals, the Marshals of France. After 1808 an entire imperial nobility was created with princes, dukes, counts and barons. If the recipients of these new honours had a large enough income their title could be made hereditary.

3 Members of the Senate were given large country estates with an annual income and the appointment as prefect in their region.

4 At the lower end of the social scale, more minor army officers and government officials were given personal gifts, such as enough money to buy a house in Paris and live comfortably.

## Education

The purpose of education, according to Napoleon, was to provide France with administrators, officials and military officers. These would be recruited from the sons of the property-owning class, the Notables. Their sons were to be educated in one of the 45 lycées or elite schools established in 1802. Places were free for the sons of army officers. Additionally, about 300 secondary schools were established in the years after 1805.

In all of these, a common curriculum was taught by government-appointed teachers, using the same textbooks and standardised lessons. This system was eventually controlled by the Imperial University, established in 1808. This standardisation was designed to bind the state together – the second purpose of education – by creating a body of teachers with a common purpose who would produce a generation of children with the same outlook and attitudes.

Those who wanted a more questioning education for their children sent them to the more expensive private schools run by the Church which were allowed after the Concordat in 1802.

At the primary level, schools were run by individuals, by the Church and by local communities. They provided moral education and basic literacy and numeracy which was all ordinary people were thought to need.

Scientific study and enquiry was not encouraged and the Polytechnique established earlier in the Revolution was converted into a military academy in 1805. However, the Sorbonne and provincial universities were reopened.

## Attitude to women

The education of women was not deemed as important by either Napoleon or by France as a whole. Women were future wives and mothers who would not need to think and who could be better raised by their own mothers (see the Civil Code, page 80).

Quick quizzes at **www.hoddereducation.co.uk/myrevisionnotes**

**Whole A-level question**

Read the three sources and the question. Write notes assessing the value of each source, using headings such as 'content and knowledge', 'provenance' and 'tone'.

With reference to these sources and your understanding of the historical context, assess the value of these three sources to an historian studying Napoleon's views on women.

## SOURCE A

Adapted extracts from the Civil Code of 1804 on the subject of Divorce.

229 The husband may demand divorce because of the adultery of his wife.

230 The wife may demand divorce because of adultery on the part of her husband, where he shall have kept his mistress in their communal home.

297 In case of divorce by mutual consent, neither of the parties shall be allowed to contract a new marriage until three years have elapsed from the pronunciation of the divorce.

298 In the case of divorce admitted by law on the ground adultery, the guilty party shall never be permitted to marry with his/her accomplice. The adulteress wife shall be condemned in the same judgement; and, on the request of the public prosecutor, to confinement in a house of correction, for a fixed period, which shall not be less than three months, nor should exceed two years.

302 The children shall be entrusted to the married Party who has obtained the divorce, unless the court, on petition of the family, or by the commissioner of government, gives order, for the greater benefit of the children, that all or some of them shall be committed to the care either of the other married party, or of a third person.

## SOURCE B

From a letter written by Napoleon to his wife Josephine from Warsaw, 23 January 1807.

I have received your letter of January 15. I can't possibly allow a woman to make the journey here. The roads are too bad – unsafe and deep in mud. Go back to Paris; be happy and cheerful; and perhaps I will come back soon. Your remark, that you married a husband in order to live with him, makes me smile. I thought in my ignorance, that the wife was made for the husband, and the husband for the country, the family and glory. Forgive my ignorance. There is always something one can learn from the fine ladies of today.

Good-bye, my dear. Remember how much it costs me not to let you come. Say to yourself, its shows how much he cares for me.

## SOURCE C

Extracts from a note written by Napoleon, concerning the curriculum for the school set up at Ecouen for the education of girls whose father, grandfather or great-grandfather had been awarded the Legion of Honour, 15 May 1807.

What are the girls brought up at Ecouen going to be taught? You must begin with religion in all its strictness. Don't allow any compromise on this point. Religion is an all important matter in a public school for girls. Whatever people may say, it is the mother's surest safeguard, and the husband's. What we ask of education is not that girls should think, but that they should believe. The weakness of women's brains, the instability of their ideas, the place they will fill in society, their need for perpetual resignation, and for an easy and generous type of charity – all this can only be met by religion, …

In addition the girls must be taught writing, arithmetic, and elementary French, so that they may know how to spell; and they ought to learn a little history and geography: but care must be taken not to let them see any Latin, or other foreign languages. The elder girls can be taught a little botany, and be taken through an easy course of physics or natural history.

# Censorship and propaganda and the Catholic Church

## Censorship and propaganda

Napoleon's regime wanted to control what was published in France. Napoleon understood the power of the press. He said, 'Four hostile newspapers are more to be feared than a thousand bayonets.' In January 1800, 60 Parisian newspapers were closed. By the end of the year four more had been shut down, leaving just nine. By 1811 there were only four, each with their own censor. Editors were expected to avoid controversial subjects and to rely for their news on the official government publications, especially its journal *Le Moniteur*. Provincial newspapers were subjected to similar censorship and control.

All other publications – books, plays, lectures and posters – were reported on and censored. Napoleon himself received daily reports, reflecting the importance he attached to this. Publications had to be sent by publishers to police headquarters for approval prior to publication. By 1810 there was a formal system of censors. All this was backed by punishments such as the closing of newspapers, printing presses and theatres, alongside punishments of offending authors, book sellers, poets and playwrights by exile, imprisonment or even, in some circumstances, death.

### The Cult of Napoleon

At the same time, Napoleon utilised the propaganda value of the visual arts. As well as buildings and the 'Empire' style, he utilised painters, notably the French artist Jacques-Louis David, to depict him in carefully controlled heroic style. For example the iconic painting 'Napoleon Crossing the Alps' depicts Napoleon on a prancing stallion, whereas in reality he crossed the Alps riding a mule.

## The position of the Church

Napoleon recognised the need to resolve the crucial conflict between the Catholic Church and the state. Since the attacks of the Revolutionary period it had regained its strength and influence on the people of France, if not its lands. Churches had been reopened and priests were holding services. Moreover, it had become identified with royalism.

## The Concordat and its aftermath

Negotiations with the Papacy began in 1800 and culminated in the Concordat, signed in 1801, published in April 1802. Under its terms:
● the Catholic Church recognised the Revolution and agreed to not try and regain its lands
● the Church was to be state-controlled, with its clergy appointed and paid by the government, to which they had to swear loyalty
● toleration of other faiths, including Jews, was to be allowed.

To this agreement Napoleon added the 'Organic Articles', which limited Papal control over French bishops while increasing the French government's control over priests.

With the Concordat Napoleon secured a tax-paying Church obedient to the state. The threat of royalism was reduced. In 1806, despite Papal objections, he even felt able to amend the Church **catechisms** to teach the people to revere and obey Napoleon himself. He went so far as to create a new St Napoleon's Day on the 16 August, the day after his birthday, to be celebrated throughout his Empire, thus adding to the Cult of Napoleon.

**Identify relevant content**

Read Source A and the question. Go through the source and highlight the sections that are relevant for the focus of the question, and annotate in the margin the main points.

How valuable is the source to explain what Napoleon gained from the Concordat?

## SOURCE A

Adapted extracts from the Concordat between the French Government and His Holiness Pius VII.

The Government of the French Republic recognises that the Roman Catholic religion is the religion of the great majority of French citizens.

**Item 4** The First Consul of the Republic shall make appointments to the archbishoprics and bishoprics of the new organisation of sees. His Holiness shall confer the canonical institution, following the forms established in relation to France before the change of Government.

**Item 6** Before taking office the bishops shall take directly, at the hands of the First Consul, the oath of loyalty to the Government.

**Item 13** His Holiness, in the interest of peace and the happy reestablishment of the Catholic religion, declares that neither he nor his successors will disturb in any manner the purchasers of the alienated ecclesiastical estates, and that, in consequence, the ownership of these same estates, the rights and revenues attached to them, shall remain in their hands and in those of their assigns.

 **Judgements on the value of a source**　　a

Read Source B and then the alternative answers that reflect the provenance of the source. Which answer will gain a higher level in the mark scheme, and why?

How valuable is the source for the historian exploring how censorship worked in Napoleonic France?

> The source is valuable to a historian investigating how Napoleon's regime worked, because it is Napoleon's own instructions to his Minister of Police.

> The source is partially valuable to a historian investigating how Napoleon's regime worked, because it is Napoleon's own instructions to his Minister of Police. However, it is less useful for revealing the extent to which Napoleon's concerns were justified or whether his instructions on censorship were actually carried out. He later dismissed his Minister of Police, Fouché.

## SOURCE B

Extract from a letter by Napoleon to Joseph Fouché, Minister of Police, 5 April 1800.

The Consuls of the Republic intend that *Le Bien Informé, Hommes Libres*, and *Défenseurs de la Patrie* shall cease publication, unless the proprietors procure editors of good character and of incorruptible patriotism. You must insist that every issue of these journals is signed by a recognised editor.

You are to instruct the Prefect of Police to take whatever steps are necessary:
1 To prevent bill-posting on the walls of Paris, or any crying of papers or pamphlets without a police licence; ...

The Prefect of the Police is to forbid the public announcement of any play, unless the Director of the theatre has a permit from the Minister of Home Affairs.

# Legal and administrative change

## The Napoleonic codes

### The Civil Code, 21 March 1804

The legal system that emerged from the Revolution was reformed by the Civil Code. This was a clear statement of the law and Napoleon was actively involved in the debates on its formulation in the Senate, although he did not always get his own way. It can be viewed as having two strands, one liberal confirming some of the changes of the Revolution and one illiberal.

It confirmed:

- the legal rights of those who had bought land confiscated from the Church and nobility
- the system of inheritance, **partage**, introduced by the Revolution
- abolition of feudalism
- equality before the law
- freedom of conscience
- the removal of the privileges of the Catholic Church.

It also:

- permitted the reintroduction of slavery in French colonies
- made workers subject to police control with the livret.

### Attitude to women

It also reversed women's rights as it:

- allowed a man to send an adulterous wife or a defiant child to prison
- made divorce expensive and difficult to obtain – in Paris, roughly 60 divorces per year were permitted.

### Napoleonic Code, 1807

The Civil Code was renamed the Napoleonic Code when it was introduced to other parts of the Empire.

## The prefects, police and control

Napoleon's control of France was maintained by a police system under the Minister of Police – for much of his reign, Joseph Fouché. The general police had wide powers and responsibilities which included monitoring public opinion and food prices in Paris, the surveillance of possible subversives, and searching for and arresting army deserters and draft dodgers and enemy agents. They were backed by gendarmes whose task was the maintenance of law and order. All reported to the Minister, who in turn sent daily reports to Napoleon.

This system of surveillance was backed by changes to the judicial system. Judges were appointed by the government for life instead of being elected and those whose loyalty was suspect were purged. This gave central government control over verdicts and sentencing. Additionally, new Criminal, Commercial and Penal Codes were published and new prisons were built.

In the departments, as well as their other administrative functions, the prefects were expected to monitor public opinion and report suspicious political activity. They could place under house arrest anyone who was viewed as a danger but who had not done anything serious enough to warrant imprisonment.

These measures, combined with those of bribes and patronage, censorship and propaganda, enabled Napoleon to control France.

## Administrative change

Administrative functions were centralised. In February 1800 Napoleon appointed prefects to take charge of each of the 83 departments of France. They were subject to the control of the Minister of the Interior. In each department there was also a council which had some influence. With their sub-prefects, the prefects supervised the police, hospitals, tax collection, conscription, village affairs and public works. Villages or communes had mayors but all local officials were appointed by the prefect.

**Diamond nine**

Read the question and complete each of the diamond nine cards with a sentence of explanation.

Then prioritise the factors by adding numbers to each diamond card or, if you have copied and cut them out, by arranging them into a diamond nine with the most important factor at the top and the least important at the bottom.

How important was Napoleon's use of patronage in ensuring that his regime had support?

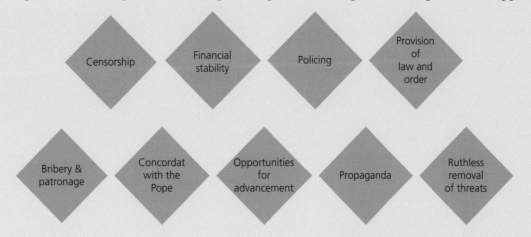

**Introducing and concluding an argument**

Look at the key points of the answer.
- How good is the proposed introduction?
- How effective is the proposed conclusion?
- Could either be improved – especially in relation to Level 5 answers?

'The features of democratic government in the constitution of 1799 were undermined in the period 1804–14.' Assess the validity of this view.

**Key points:**
- Limited nature of democratic involvement.
- Increasing control of the Senate by Napoleon using: i) patronage, ii) original 60 members increased by his appointees/own supporters to 80 and finally to over 100.
- Increased use of the police and censorship to limit public discussion.

**Introduction:**

The features of democratic government in the constitution of 1799 were not that extensive to begin with. Democratic involvement in elections was limited as voters were selecting candidates from a limited number of choices. Meanwhile the plebiscites that were held had limited turn outs and were rigged in places. However, the constitution provided the Senate, Tribunate and Legislature as a balance to the power of the First Consul and over time Napoleon was able to reduce these to the position of willing supporters of his policies by using a number of strategies.

**Conclusion:**

In conclusion, the features of democratic government in the constitution of 1799 were undermined by Napoleon in the period 1804–14.

# Financial and economic policies and problems, part 1

In 1799, with the Directory's major source of funding plunder from occupied countries cut off, the government treasury was almost empty and its debts amounted to over 450 million francs. Napoleon made reforms to rationalise and stabilise government funding. This included the appointment of able men who were kept in post long term.

## Reforming government ministries

- The Ministry of the Treasury, headed by Francois Barbé-Marbois, was responsible for government expenditure.
- The Ministry of Finances, headed by Martin Gaudin up to 1814, was responsible for the collection of taxation and revenues.
- An Audit Office was set up in 1807 to check on all government spending.

## Taxation

Gaudin took control of the assessment and collection of direct taxes away from local authorities. His centralised control led to great improvements. The main direct tax was the land tax. Land registers showing ownership were drawn up and the tax registers showing who should pay were improved. These steps made its collection fair and efficient. Throughout the period the land tax provided 29 per cent of all government income – but it did not need to be increased, which would have upset Napoleon's key supporters.

Instead, indirect taxes were increased to pay for war. In 1804 responsibility for the collection of indirect taxes on goods was given to a central excise office. As well as continuing the unpopular taxes on goods initiated by the Directory, new ones were added on wine, playing cards and, most controversially in 1806, on salt. Income from these increased by over 400 per cent between 1806 and 1812 so that they came to provide 25 per cent of government income.

## The central economy

### The Bank of France

This was founded by Napoleon in 1800 as a private bank, but it had a range of public functions, including the sole right to issue paper notes. Later, it had strict controls placed upon its actions. Having a central bank made the government's task of raising finance much easier, something the Ancien Régime crucially lacked.

### Currency

Napoleon introduced a new currency, the franc de germinal, based upon gold and silver coins. He was depicted on them in the style of a Roman Emperor. Strict control of the metal content ensured that this was a stable currency which provided a strong base for the French economy, something that the Revolutionary paper based assignat had failed to do.

### Industry

The cotton industry grew dramatically due to:
- the mechanisation of spinning, using copies of British machines
- increased demand
- no competition from British cloth as a result of the war.

Other textile industries declined.

The chemical industry made some developments in connection with textiles and soap making. Meanwhile, the iron industry benefited from the demand for war armaments but did not make significant technological advances.

### Agriculture

There were no changes in farming methods and little investment. The only change was the growing of sugar beet and chicory to replace the colonial imports of sugar and coffee cut off by the war.

**Develop the detail** a

Below are a sample exam question and a paragraph written in answer to this question. The paragraph contains a limited amount of detail. Annotate the paragraph to add additional detail to the answer.

How successful was Napoleon in achieving financial stability for the French Government in the years 1804–14?

Between 1804 and 1814 Napoleon and his government took a number of steps to ensure the financial stability of his regime. New ministries and offices were set up and new ministers were appointed. The Bank of France was set up in 1800 and Napoleon supported and controlled this. The centralisation of government allowed Napoleon to make a number of changes to the tax system, both direct and indirect taxes, with the result that more tax income was raised. He also brought in a new currency based upon metal rather than paper. Altogether these measures led to more stable government finances.

 **Identify relevant content**

Read Source A and the question below. Go through the source and highlight the sections that are relevant for the focus of the question, and annotate in the margin the main points.

How valuable is the source for the historian investigating Napoleon's financial and economic problems?

## SOURCE A

An extract from the memoires of Marie-Victoire Monnard, who set up in business as a draper in Paris in the 1790s.

The *assignats*, the paper currency of the time, were losing value and gave to whoever wanted the chance to open a shop with little merchandise. A few samples were enough to buy and sell. That gave me the idea of setting up on my own. I told my father, explaining the advantages I had in mind; he wasn't opposed, but did not give me any money to get started … But, to begin a small business, one has to have either some goods or the money to buy them; having neither the one nor the other I cut my sheets into towels because they were too coarse for anything else; I sold them, as well as a nankeen dress with wide stripes that I still had, plus a pillow. I earned in total about 40 francs and used them to buy ten lengths of calico, which I immediately sold, making 8 francs profit. I was so happy with this beginning to my business that I would not have given up my position for that of the greatest ruler in the world. The continued decline in the value of the *assignats* facilitated the sale of all kinds of merchandise; they only had to be put up for sale and they were sold.

# Financial and economic policies and problems, part 2

## The impact of war and the Continental System

France was at war from 1803 to 1814, but the one opponent Napoleon was unable to defeat was Britain, protected as it was by its control of the seas, secured after the **Battle of Trafalgar** in 1805. Thereafter the British fleet was able to blockade French ports. This led to a decline in the seaport economy linked to cities such as Bordeaux and Nantes.

## The Continental System

The Continental System was designed by Napoleon as an economic attack on Britain. It was announced in the Berlin Decrees in November 1806 and extended in 1807 by the Milan Decrees. The decrees forbade any trade with Britain by France and the other satellite states in Napoleon's empire. Napoleon hoped that by stopping British exports and re-exports to the continent its economy and industries would be damaged. At the same time, allowing Britain to continue to import goods, but only with cash payment, would deplete the British economy still further, thus rendering Britain unable to continue the war. This would have the added benefit of protecting French industries from British competition both in France and in selling to the rest of the Empire.

## Effects on France

The decline in the seaport economy included not just trade but also related industries such as ship building and rope making. Other French industries that relied upon export markets also suffered. However, in central and eastern France, trade routes along the Rhine and across the Alps opened new markets both in the Empire and bordering territories.

## Effects on Britain

To begin with, the lack of French sea power hampered the effectiveness of the System. In 1809, in a twin-pronged policy, Napoleon improved efforts to seize and destroy smuggled goods and at the same time started to licence some trade with Britain, in grain and wine. Historians differ on how badly Britain was affected. Some argue that it was very little, with new markets developing in North and South America, while others suggest that in 1811 Britain's trade with the continent fell by as much as 50 per cent. Undoubtedly, Britain's efforts to counter-blockade France was one cause of the **Anglo–American War of 1812**.

## Effects on Europe

The Continental System created tensions between Napoleon and some of the states within his Empire, as well as those outside. For example, Portugal's refusal to take part led to the Peninsular War, beginning in 1808, while Russia's withdrawal precipitated Napoleon's invasion of 1812.

## Degree of economic change

Overall, the French economy stood still in the period 1800–15. Growth in some areas was balanced by decline in others. However, Napoleon did leave a legacy of new canals and spent 277 million francs on roads, including the requirement that they be protected from the sun by the planting of trees along them.

**Whole A-level question**

Read the three sources and the question. Write notes assessing the value of each source, using headings such as 'content and knowledge', 'provenance' and 'tone'.

With reference to these sources and your understanding of the historical context, assess the value of these three sources to a historian studying the workings of Napoleon's Continental System.

## SOURCE A

Extracts from the Berlin Decree, 21 November 1806. The Berlin Decree signed by Napoleon set out the rules of the Continental System.

Article 1. The British Isles are declared to be in a state of blockade.

Article 2. All commerce and all correspondence with the British Isles is forbidden.

Article 3. Every individual who is an English subject, of whatever state or condition he may be, found in any country occupied by Our troops or by those of Our allies, shall be made a prisoner of war.

Article 4. All warehouses, merchandise or property of whatever kind belonging to a subject of England shall be regarded as a lawful prize.

Article 5. Trade in English goods is prohibited, and all goods belonging to England, or coming from her factories or her colonies, are declared a lawful prize.

Article 7. No vessel coming directly from England or from the English colonies shall be received in any port.

Article 10. The present decree shall be communicated by Our minister of foreign affairs to the King of Spain, Naples, Holland and Etruria, and to Our other allies whose subjects, like Ours, are the victims of the injustice and the barbarity of English maritime legislation.

## SOURCE B

A note from Lord Howick, British Secretary of State of Foreign Affairs, to Mr Monroe, an American diplomat, dated 10 January 1807.

The undersigned, His Majesty's principal Secretary of State of Foreign Affairs, has received His Majesty's commands to acquaint Mr Monroe that the French Government having issued certain orders, which, in violation of the usages of war, purport to prohibit the commerce of all neutral nations with His Majesty's dominions, and also to prevent such nations from trading with any other country in any articles, the growth, produce, or manufacture of His Majesty's dominions. And the said Government having also taken upon itself to declare all His Majesty's dominions to be in a state of blockade, at a time when the fleets of France and her allies are themselves confined within their own ports by the superior valor and discipline of the British navy.

## SOURCE C

Adapted from a letter by Napoleon to Prince Eugène, Viceroy of Italy, 23 August 1810.

I have received your letter of August 14. All the raw silk from the Kingdom of Italy goes to England, for there are no silk factories in Germany. It is therefore quite natural that I should wish to divert it from this route to the advantage of my French manufacturers. Otherwise my silk factories, one of the chief supports of French commerce, would suffer substantial losses. I cannot agree with your observations. My principle is France first. You must never lose sight of the fact that, if English commerce is supreme on the high seas, it is due to her sea power. It is therefore to be expected that, as France is the strongest land power, she should claim commercial supremacy on the continent. It is indeed our only hope. And isn't it better for Italy to come to the help of France, in such an important matter as this? ... It would be short-sighted not to recognise that Italy owes her independence to France; that it was won by French blood and French victories.

# Exam focus

On pages 88–89 is a sample Level 5 answer to an A-level question on source evaluation. Read the answer and the comments around it.

With reference to Sources A, B and C and your understanding of the historical context, assess the value of these three sources to an historian studying the concerns and working of the Napoleonic state in France in its early years.

## SOURCE A

Adapted from Lucien Bonaparte's address as Minister of the Interior to the newly appointed prefects explaining their role, February 1800. He had appointed many of them.

This post demands a wide range of duties, but it offers you great rewards in the future: you have been summoned to assist the government in its noble design to restore France to her ancient splendour, and to establish this magnificent edifice on the unshakable foundations of liberty and equality ... You will not be called upon to carry out the whims or passing desires of a fickle government, unstable in its operation, and anxious about its future. Your first task is to destroy irrevocably, in your department, the influence of those events which for too long have dominated our minds. Do your utmost to bring hatred and passion to an end, to extinguish rancour, to blot out the painful memories of the past ...

Do not tolerate any public reference to the labels which still cling to the diverse political parties of the revolution; merely consign them to that most deplorable chapter in the history of human folly ...

You will receive from the War Minister all the instructions necessary for the administrative responsibilities within his jurisdiction. I will simply limit myself to a reminder to apply yourself immediately to the conscription draft. I give special priority to the collection of taxes: their prompt payment is now a sacred duty.

## SOURCE B

From a report by the sub-Prefect of Nyons in the Drôme Department, 23 January 1802.

Brigandage which has devastated this region for such a long time, which exiled peace and security for several years, being almost completely defeated, its impure remains have dared, to make new attacks against the public security of this *arrondissement*. The presence of a few of these bandits who, sometimes, are still seen, no longer alarm citizens assured of rapid and effective protection, and who are full of confidence in the wisdom, activity and zeal of the higher authorities of the department. If the inhabitants of the countryside removed from the provincial capital have not come out strongly against the brigands, and suffer them in their midst, it is the result of ignorance which renders their coarse spirits more susceptible of impressions of fear and terror, or of a simplicity which it is easy to take advantage of. The surest and most customary means is to pass oneself off as a deserter. It is by means of this disguise that the brigands find shelter in the mountains of this *arrondissement*, without arousing mistrust or suspicion.

## SOURCE C

Instructions for Senators written by Napoleon at Saint Cloud, 28 March 1805. They were to visit their departments by a set date on the pretext of examining their estates.

Actually your most important duty will be to supply Us with trustworthy and positive information on any point which may interest the government; and to this end, you will send Us a direct report, once a week, from the capital town of your department.
1  You are to discover what is the character, conduct and capacity of public officials, both in the administrative and judicial departments.
2  What principles the clergy hold, and how much influence they have.
3  Who the leading men are in each part of your arrondissement, in virtue of their character, wealth, opinions, and popular influence; and to what class of society they belong.
4  You will investigate, in the different classes and cantons, the state of public opinion on: (i) the government; (ii) religion; (iii) conscription; (iv) the road tax; (v) the incidence of indirect taxation.
5  You will notice whether there are any persons in hiding from conscription; if so, how many; and whether a rising of any kind is to be feared from this cause.

Source A is particularly valuable as it shows the historian the thoughts of Lucien Bonaparte, Napoleon's brother, who played such an important role in the coup of Brumaire. Napoleon appointed him as his Minister of the Interior, and at this stage the brothers were working closely together, so it gives us a very good insight into the thoughts and concerns of the regime in its early stages. The two were later to fall out. The prefects were an important part of government. Their job was to oversee each of the 83 departments for the central government and, as the source says, they had wide powers including the appointment of the local officials who served under them. So, the source tells us about their functions but it also reveals some of the concerns of Napoleon's regime, what it was worried about and what it thought was important.

> A good start. There is an immediate focus on the provenance of the source, backed by contextual knowledge and a summation of what the source is useful for.

In terms of the functions of the prefects, it makes clear that they have to follow the instructions of Napoleon's Minister of the Interior but also those of the Minister of War. This helps support the argument that since the revolution the French state had been mobilised for total war, with the Minister of War having wide-reaching powers. The specific example here is conscription. The provision of men for the army is clearly crucial to Napoleon's Italian campaign. Later, in 1800, he won the crushing victory over the Austrians at Marengo and cleared them out of Italy. The other matter which is also important is the collection of taxes. The centralisation of administration was essential to the success of Napoleon's regime, something Louis XVI's Ancien Régime had been unable to achieve. The prefects appointed all local officials and were in charge of the police, hospitals and public works.

> This paragraph links with the introduction, focuses upon content and makes good use of contextual knowledge.

Where this source is really valuable is in what it reveals about the regime's concerns. This is early in the regime, when Napoleon's position was not yet secure. He was still only First Consul at this date. In terms of motivating the prefects and keeping them loyal to Napoleon, it is noticeable that they are being offered great rewards. One way in which the Napoleonic state worked was through patronage. Although the Legion of Honour was not started until 1804, the source seems to be suggesting some sort of honours, as it talks about noble designs and restoring ancient splendour. The rewards could easily be the titles and lands that were later used to reward soldiers and administrators like the prefects.

> The candidate is starting to explore the tone of the address and linking it to future developments in Napoleon's regime.

Where Source A is most valuable is how it shows Lucien's, and probably Napoleon's, views on the Directory regime that they overthrew. The tone is very judgemental, describing the 'whims' of a 'fickle government' and offering a summary of its weakness in that it is 'unstable' and 'anxious'. He is really talking about the weaknesses in the constitution on which the Directory was based, with the annual elections and potential for the balance of power to become a stalemate. Of course, it would have been odd if the writer had been more positive. Finally, the instability of the Consulship is apparent in the concern to control past arguments. The Directory had been plagued by disputes between royalists and neo-Jacobins and this is something Napoleon and his government were anxious to stop – hence the instruction to the prefects to not tolerate public use of those labels such as 'royalist'. So, the source is more valuable for what it does not overtly say but rather for what can be read into it.

> This paragraph is most effective. It refers to both the provenance and tone in order to judge the value of the source.

On the surface, Source B is less valuable. It is the report of a sub-prefect, so someone who will know what is going on in their district. However, they are writing a report for a superior so they have an obvious motive to present themselves and their work in the best possible light. They write about how brigandage had 'devastated this region' before it was 'almost completely defeated'. The historian can learn that brigandage is again a problem in 1802, but the extent of that problem is more difficult to determine. The sub-prefect says that there are just a 'few'. He also goes on to blame the ignorance and simplicity of the people. The additional problem is how representative this region is of France as a whole. It does mention mountains which are often more lawless regions. So, all this lessens the value of this source on its own.

However, two interesting pieces of information are contained within it. The first is that lawlessness is more likely to be found further from the centre of power, the provincial capital where the prefect would probably be found. This may hold true across France. The second is that conscription and army service were not universally popular in France. It provoked the revolt in the Vendée during the revolution in the first place and led to that revolt reigniting on a number of occasions. In 1802 the problem is such that someone pretending to be a deserter from the army is likely to get sympathy rather than criticism and that is why brigands are using it as a disguise for themselves. This makes the source quite valuable.

Source C is undoubtedly another valuable source because these are instructions from Napoleon himself to senators and it is secret advice. They are to pretend to be visiting their estates while really they are reporting back to Napoleon himself, the 'Us'. This adds to the evidence for a historian that surveillance was one of the ways in which Napoleon kept control of his Empire. He is Emperor by this date. Three groups of people are clearly under watch here – public officials, the clergy and leading men. The first group would be part of the government, making sure everything is working properly. Providing law and order was one of the things that made Napoleon's regime popular, especially after the disorder of the later years of the Directory, something Source B drew attention to. More interesting is his continuing concern with the clergy and the previous links between royalism and the Catholic Church. Although the Concordat with the Pope had been agreed in 1802, this did not mean that all the clergy had stepped into line – this is clear from Napoleon's asking about their views and their influence. The commonly held view is that his grip on power is secure once he is crowned Emperor in 1804 but this source reveals to the historian that there are still dangers – this is reinforced by the third point of enquiry into the views of leading men. The French revolutionaries from the 1790s onwards were very concerned with plots, conspiracies and rebellions, and the Bourbons and their supporters were still there as a threat. In 1804 there was the plot to murder Napoleon and replace him with the Duc d'Enghien. Finally, the source reveals that avoiding conscription as mentioned in Source B remains a problem.

This paragraph is less effective. It explores both the provenance and tone to judge the value of the source. It fails to exploit the linkage to context such as the breakdown in law and order towards the end of the Directory and the role of the gendarmerie in addressing this under Napoleon.

This paragraph is most effective in picking up on the content and what it reveals and makes the link across time, albeit without using precise supporting information.

This paragraph is impressive. It covers all the strands at a high level. The brief cross-reference to Sources B and A shows total command of the content of the three sources.

This is a very strong and lengthy answer, albeit lacking a formal conclusion. The assessment of all three sources is impressive, with comments on the importance of provenance, tone and the content of the sources. The contextual knowledge is also strong. This is a Level 5 response.

### Reverse engineering

The best essays are based on careful plans. Read the essay and the comments and try to work out the general points of the plan used to write the essay. Once you have done this, note down the specific examples used to support each general point.

# 6 The impact of Napoleon's rule on Europe, 1799–1815

## The army and conquest during the Consulate and Empire, part 1

REVISED

Napoleon needed a military success to consolidate his Consulship. He crossed the Alps and defeated the Austrians at Marengo in June 1800. This enhanced his popularity, but the Austrians were only willing to negotiate peace after General Moreau's victory at Hohenlinden in Bavaria in December 1800. With the Second Coalition destroyed, England was prepared to negotiate. The Peace of Amiens was agreed in March 1802, but did not last. In the interim Napoleon failed to recapture the Caribbean colony of Saint-Domingue and sold Louisiana to the United States.

### The War of the Third Coalition, 1803–06

War – The Napoleonic Wars – broke out again in May 1803 and the Third Coalition had formed by 1805. The Russian Tsar was angry at the shooting of the Duc d'Enghien and French actions in Germany while the Austrians were angered by French expansion in Italy. Napoleon's British invasion plans were destroyed by defeat at Trafalgar in October 1805. In the following three months he won a swift series of victories over the Austrians at Ulm in October 1805 and the Austrians and Russians at Austerlitz in December 1805. The Russians retreated, while Austria agreed a separate peace giving France control of Northern Italy.

### The War of the Fourth Coalition, 1806–07

War with Prussia was provoked by Napoleon's attempts to impose his Continental System and expanding influence in Germany. Prussia was decisively defeated in the battles of Jena and Auerstadt, October 1806. Thereafter Napoleon advanced through Poland to attack Russia and won the battles of Eylau, February 1807, and Friedland, June 1807. The real significance of Eylau with it great slaughter was that it showed Russia could withstand his attack. Nevertheless, Napoleon was able on this occasion to force Russia's Tsar Alexander I and Prussia to negotiate the Treaty of Tilsit, July 1807. This essentially divided Europe between the French and Russian Empires.

## Reasons for military success by 1808

### The part played by Napoleon

Napoleon was an able general.
- He inspired personal devotion from his troops, utilising such devices as his Bulletins and Order of the Days.
- He organised the French armies to combine flexibility with central command, for example corps of 25,000–30,000 men. This was crucial for following up victories swiftly to make them decisive.
- He utilised new aggressive tactics such as deploying infantry in lines or columns and making units on the march independent so they could live off the land and move quickly.
- He controlled every detail. He ordered and his generals obeyed.
- He made good decisions on the battlefield – for example, at Austerlitz.

### The weaknesses of his enemies

- The superior combined forces of the coalitions were continually hampered by their failure to co-ordinate. Often they pursued their separate aims.
- Their armies lacked good artillery and their tactics were old fashioned and static.

### The strength of the Grande Armée

This was created by Napoleon between 1801 and 1805, building upon the mass conscript armies of the Revolution. Its size, morale, organisation and enthusiasm was superior to that of any of the enemies it faced and its officers were better, as a result of promotion by merit.

**Delete as applicable**

Below are a sample exam question and a paragraph written as an answer. Read the paragraph and decide which of the possible options (in bold) is most appropriate. Complete the paragraph by justifying your selection.

How successful were Napoleon's foreign policies during the Consulate?

*Napoleon's foreign policy during the Consulate was successful to a **great/fair/limited** extent. For example, he crossed the Alps and defeated the Austrians at Marengo June 1800 although the Austrians were only willing to negotiate peace after General Moreau's victory at Hohenlinden in December 1800. With the Second Coalition destroyed England was prepared to agree the Peace of Amiens in March 1802, but this did not last. In the interim Napoleon failed to recapture the Caribbean colony of Saint-Domingue, sold Louisiana to the United States and agreed the Concordat with the Pope. In this way, Napoleon's policy was **extremely/moderately/slightly** successful because*

_____

_____

 **Judgements on the value of a source**

Read Source A below and then the alternative answers that reflect the provenance and content of the source. Which answer will gain the higher level in the mark scheme, and why? How could you improve that answer?

> *The source is valuable to a historian investigating the problems faced by Napoleon in controlling his Empire, because it shows his troops were not always welcomed.*

> *The source is partially valuable to a historian investigating the problems faced by Napoleon in controlling his Empire. It shows that his occupation forces did face local opposition and suggests, as the original booksellers are Austrian, that Austria was behind this. It does not show how serious a threat this opposition was but the severity of the punishment – death – suggests that Napoleon judged it to be a very serious threat.*

## SOURCE A

Extract from a letter from Napoleon to one of his commanders, Marshall Berthier, 5 August 1806, during the War of the Fourth Coalition. Here Napoleon outlines his plan for those who oppose his occupation of Germany.

I imagine that you have arrested the Augsburg and Nuremberg booksellers. My intention is to bring them before a court-martial, and to have them shot within 24 hours. It is no ordinary crime to spread defamatory writings in places occupied by the French armies, and to incite the inhabitants against them. It is high treason. The sentence must declare that, since, wherever an army may be, it is the duty of its commander to see to its safety, such and such individuals, having been found guilty of trying to rouse the inhabitants of Swabia against the French army, are condemned to death.

You will parade the guilty men in the centre of a division, and appoint seven colonels to be their judges. In the sentence, you must mention that the defamatory writings originally came from the booksellers Kupfer of Vienna and Enrich of Linz, and they are condemned to death in their absence, the sentence to be carried out, if they are captured, wherever the French troops may happen to be. You are to have the sentence published all over Germany.

# The army and conquest during the Consulate and Empire, part 2

## The 'Grand Empire'

By 1807 Napoleon was victorious, France dominated Europe, and the Empire was created. In the next four years smaller states were added until the Empire reached its greatest extent by 1811. It consisted of:

● France up to its 'natural frontiers' – the Alps, Pyrenees and River Rhine, including Belgium
● annexed territories – Piedmont (1802), Swiss Confederation (1803), Ligurian Republic (1805) and the Grand Duchy of Tuscany (1809)
● satellite states – kingdoms of Italy (1805), Naples (1806), Holland (1806), Westphalia (1807), Spain (1808), the Confederation of the Rhine (1806) and the Grand Duchy of Warsaw (1807).

## The reasons for expansion and the building of an empire

The Empire was created initially to protect Revolutionary France from attack by the monarchies of Europe – Austria, Britain, Prussia and Russia. Beyond that, historians differ on Napoleon's motives. Some point to his desire to implement the Civil Code in other territories and to giving people their freedom from oppressive governments, some to his personal lust for power and glory, others to his enduring hatred of Britain – while others see him as simply trying to strengthen his position. In his writings he shows a preoccupation with the notion of a universal empire. His choice of the title King of Rome for his son makes apparent a connection to the **Holy Roman Empire** and the empire of Charlemagne.

## The value and problems of the Grand Empire

The annexed territories were treated as part of France with the same rights and obligations as any other region. Like them, they provided tax income and soldiers.

The satellite states were treated differently. They were expected to pay tribute and to provide auxiliary soldiers for the Grande Armée. Members of Napoleon's family were placed on their thrones. This had the twin benefit of ensuring their loyalty and rewarding his family. Finally they were a useful source of lands and estates, taken from their original nobility or the Church, which Napoleon could give as rewards to his new nobility and to his leading marshals and generals.

Together with his beaten enemies, the satellite states provided roughly half Napoleon's military expenditure from 1804 to 1814, as well as financing the auxiliary troops they had been forced to provide.

### Problems

The Empire was not universally popular. Conscription, in particular, was hated and resisted, but there was armed rebellion in only three regions – Calabria in Naples, the Tyrol in Austria, and Spain.

The scale of the Empire was a problem in itself. Napoleon used members of his own family, but there were only so many of them – and not all were both competent and loyal. For example, Napoleon moved his brother Joseph from Naples to Spain and replaced him with his brother-in-law, Marshall Murat. Murat later conspired against Napoleon. To the north, Napoleon's brother Louis refused to implement the Continental Blockade in Holland, while in Sweden, Marshall Bernadotte turned against his old master.

## ! Complete the paragraph   a

Below are a sample exam question and a paragraph written in answer to this question. The paragraph contains a point and some specific examples. Can you add any more?

It also lacks a concluding analytical link back to the question. Complete the paragraph, adding this link back to the question in the space provided.

How successful was Napoleon's use of family members to control his Grand Empire?

Napoleon placed members of his family in control of some parts of his Grand Empire. For example, he made his brothers kings — Louis in Holland and Joseph in Spain. He believed that he could rely upon their family loyalty, which on the whole he could. His sister and her husband, Murat, who Napoleon placed on the throne of Naples, did conspire against him. However, his family members did not always follow his policies, as when Joseph was reluctant to enforce the Continental System in Holland. Nevertheless, the lack of rebellions against his rule across the Empire suggests that even if they did not always have Napoleon's approval they did at least rule without causing major problems. Overall,

_____

_____

## i Moving from assertion to argument   a

Below are a sample exam question and a series of assertions forming a part answer. Read the exam question and then add a justification to each of the assertions to turn it into an argument.

'The size of Napoleon's Grand Empire was more a strength than a weakness.' Assess the validity of this view.

Napoleon's Grand Empire was large because ...

... and this meant that ...

Napoleon was able to make use of family members and trusted Generals to run parts of his Empire and this was ...

When Napoleon invaded Russia in 1812 he was able to do so with an army of 600,000 men. This was because ...

# The control of the Grand Empire

## Pacification

In the period 1800–05 the only fighting that took place was at sea or in the colonies. On the continent there was peace. Napoleon used this period to pacify and control the annexed territories. Feudalism had already been abolished in these territories during the revolutionary period. The Civil Code (Napoleonic Code) was introduced with the same civil and criminal courts and the same system of government administration with Departments, prefects and centralised control was followed. The German and Italian territories that were annexed 1806–09 had less time under French control and in them many of the changes did not last beyond Napoleon's fall in 1815.

## The control of the Grand Empire: administration

The rulers of the satellite states were closely supervised by Napoleon and they were expected to rule in France's interests. Some changes were made to their administrative structures. They were divided into departments controlled by a prefect, just as in France. Below that, the canton was abolished as an electoral unit but retained as the base for the four arms of imperial control. These were the gendarmes, who answered to the Minister of War, the mayors who, with the prefect, answered to the Minister of the Interior, the justices of the peace, who answered to the Minister of Justice and the police commissioner, who answered to the Minister of Police.

Some of the smaller states in Germany and Italy were amalgamated or joined to bigger states. This has sometimes led to Napoleon being seen as a supporter of nationalism in countries other than France, and as a contributor to the future growth of the states of Germany and Italy, but this was not his intention at the time.

### The gendarmerie

One of Napoleon's key achievements was to impose law and order throughout France and, gradually, the Empire. Gendarmes, ex-soldiers, were stationed in units of six or seven men in small rural centres, as well as in the towns. They were a visible presence of government and provided both protection and law and order.

## Financial and economic policies

The reformed French fiscal system served as a model throughout the Empire. Napoleon placed heavy financial demands on satellite states like Holland and Italy – in order to meet these they had to modernise their finances with more efficient tax collection and more careful state control.

However, considerable damage to local economies was caused by the burden of taxation, by the economic destruction associated with warfare and by French occupying troops. Moreover, conscription removed manpower from agriculture and contributed to longer-term economic decline, as did the loss of manpower dues to deaths in battle.

## Social policies

Napoleon did not abolish feudalism in all the territories he conquered. In some he adopted a pragmatic approach of exercising his power through existing elites. Historians now agree that the groupings of nobles and bourgeois remained unchanged in much of Italy, Germany and Poland.

## ! Identify relevant content

Read Source A and the question below. Go through the source and highlight the sections that are relevant for the focus of the question, and annotate in the margin the main points.

How valuable is the source for explaining the problems Napoleon faced in running his Grand Empire?

### SOURCE A

Extract from a letter by Napoleon to his brother-in-law, Joachim Murat, King of Naples, 27 November 1808.

I read with attention the memorandum submitted by your minister, secretary of state of Justice, on the Code Napoleon. The most important consideration in the Code is that of divorce; it is its foundation. You should not touch it in any manner whatsoever; it is the law of the State. I would prefer Naples to belong to the former king of Sicily than to see an expurgated Code Napoleon. Divorce is not contrary to religion; its provisions have in any case been greatly modified. Moreover, those whose consciences have been offended by it will never use it. I cannot consent, in my capacity as guarantor of the Constitution, to modifications to the Code Napoleon. It has been adopted throughout the kingdom of Italy; Florence has it, Rome will have it soon, and priests will have to cease nurturing prejudices and look to their own affairs.

## ⟐ Spectrum of importance    **a**

Below are a sample exam question and a list of changes which could be used to answer the question. Use your own knowledge and the information on the opposite page to reach a judgement about the importance of these changes. Write numbers on the spectrum below to indicate their relative importance. Having done this, write a brief justification of your placement, explaining why some of these factors are more important than others. The resulting diagram could form the basis of an essay plan.

'The most important change to the annexed states in Napoleon's Grand Empire was the abolition of feudalism.' Assess the validity of this view.

1 Abolition of feudalism

2 Conscription

3 Continental system

4 The Napoleonic Code

5 Gendarmerie

6 Fiscal and financial reforms

←                                      →

Least important                                      Most important

## The Continental Blockade

Without sea power, Napoleon was unable to defeat Britain. This meant he needed to enforce his Continental Blockade to cripple Britain's economy. To make the Blockade effective he had to not only control France and the satellite states, but also his neighbours and sometime allies. In 1808 this led to him invading Italy to make the Pope impose the Blockade, a successful invasion that gave Napoleon control of all of Italy.

## The Peninsular War, 1808–14

In May 1808, in an attempt to enforce the Blockade in Spain, Napoleon replaced the Spanish king with his brother, Joseph. This was not a success. The Spanish did not welcome the French – in Madrid they rose in a revolt, which was brutally suppressed. This led to the outbreak of guerrilla warfare, which became a major factor in France's ultimate defeat. Meanwhile, a small French army was defeated by regular Spanish troops. News of this victory spread across Europe and in response Napoleon took his Grande Armée to Spain. Before he had time to fully complete its pacification he had to turn his attention to the Austrians. He never returned to Spain but the war there dragged on until 1814.

The French faced guerrilla warfare from the Spanish, which tied down thousands of troops in garrisons and disrupted their lines of supply and communications. Plus, they faced regular warfare from the British armies, under Wellington, sent to aid their Portuguese ally in 1808. French efforts to drive the British out of Portugal in 1810–11 failed and, when the war began to turn against Napoleon across Europe, Wellington was able to move onto the attack. After a series of victories at Salamanca, 1812, and Vittoria, 1813, Spain was liberated and the French were driven back over the Pyrenees.

While not a decisive theatre of the war, this conflict was a constant drain on French resources in terms of men (over 350,000 deployed there, with estimated losses of 250,000), money, morale and prestige. Napoleon called it the 'Spanish ulcer'.

## The Austrian campaign, 1809

When Napoleon left Spain he marched to the Danube to face the Austrians. Having learnt from their previous mistakes in 1805, the Austrians had reorganised their armies, improved their artillery and appointed new generals. In April the Austrians were defeated but in May it was Napoleon who was beaten – for the first time in over a decade – at the Battle of Aspern by the Archduke Charles. The campaign was brought to an end by Napoleon's last great victory at Wagram in July. He was able to dictate the terms of the peace, which included Austria losing territory and paying an indemnity of £4 million. However, his enemies were encouraged by the fact that he personally had been defeated on the battlefield at Aspern.

Napoleon then negotiated to marry an Austrian princess, having divorced his wife Josephine. His new bride, Marie-Louise, was a niece of Marie Antoinette. She was to provide Napoleon with the heir he wanted to secure his dynasty, but the marriage also caused tension with Russia.

**Source evaluation**

Read the two sources and the question below. Write notes assessing the value of each source, using headings such as 'content and knowledge', 'provenance' and 'tone'.

Assess the value of these two sources to a historian studying Napoleon's response to challenges to his Empire.

## SOURCE A

Extract from a letter from Napoleon to General Junot, 7 February 1806, on dealing with a local rebellion in Piedmont.

I am certain that M. Moreau has badly administered, and you will see that I have recalled him and replaced him with a prefect. But that does not justify the rebellion. The report from the major of the 42nd is from a man who does not know the Italians, who are false. Seditious under a weak government, they only respect and fear a strong and active government.

My wish is that the village which rebelled so as to give itself over to Bobbo should be burned, that the priest who is in the hands of the Bishop of Plaisance be shot, and that three or four hundred of the culprits be sent to the galleys. I do not have the same notions of clemency as you. One can only be merciful by being severe, without which that unfortunate country and Piedmont would be lost, and torrents of blood would be needed to assure the tranquillity of Italy. We have known rebellion; it must be met with vengeance and punishment.

## SOURCE B

Extract from an Order of the Army, 12 December 1808, relating to the behaviour of troops in Spain.

The emperor is unhappy with the disturbances which are taking place. Pillage destroys everything, even the army which practises it. Peasants desert; it has the double inconvenience of turning them into irreconcilable enemies who get their revenge on isolated soldiers, and who swell enemy ranks as we destroy them; and of depriving us of all information, so necessary to make war, and of all means of obtaining subsistence. Peasants who used to come to the markets are kept away by the troops who arrest them, plunder their goods and beat them.

The emperor orders his marshals, generals and officers to take the firmest measures in order to put an end to these abuses and to these excesses which compromise the safety of the army. Consequently, it is ordered that:

1 Any individual who stops or mistreats an inhabitant or peasant carrying goods into the city of Madrid will be immediately tried before a military tribunal and condemned to death.

 **Recommended reading**

Below is a list of suggested further reading on challenges to the Empire.

- John Lawrence Tone, 'The Peninsular War' in *Napoleon and Europe*, pages 225–242, ed. Philip G Dwyer [2001]
- Mike Rapport, *The Napoleonic Wars: A Very Short Introduction*, pages 38–55 (2013)
- Paul Johnson, *Napoleon*, pages 51–75 (2002)
- David A Bell, *Napoleon: A Concise Biography*, pages 43–83 (2016)

### The Russian campaign, 1812

The Continental Blockade was to prove a decisive factor in the breakdown of relations between France and Russia. Tsar Alexander withdrew from it at the end of 1810. There were other sources of friction between the two:

- Napoleon's Austrian marriage
- rival ambitions to seize Turkish territory – including Istanbul, in the Balkans
- rival ambitions in the Baltic – Napoleon annexed the Duchy of Oldenburg, Alexander annexed Swedish Finland
- disagreement over the future of the Grand Duchy of Poland.

Napoleon assembled a huge army of 600,000 men. Less than half were French; the rest were drawn from throughout his Empire and from his allies. There were Austrians, Danes, Germans, Italians, Lithuanians, Prussians, Poles, Portuguese, Spanish and Swiss.

In June, Napoleon invaded Russia. Despite his victory at Borodino in September and the subsequent occupation of Moscow the Tsar refused to negotiate a peace treaty – in the end Napoleon was forced to retreat. The campaign was a disaster for a number of reasons:

- The Russians, apart from Borodino, refused to fight the formal battle that Napoleon believed would give him a decisive victory.
- The Russians adopted a scorched-earth strategy, destroying all food and supplies on Napoleon's line of march and so preventing his army living off the land as it usually did.
- Russian skirmishers constantly attacked, killing many and damaging morale.
- The Russian army was much larger.
- Napoleon lacked a clear strategic objective.
- His approach of controlling every detail could not work with such large armies.
- Poor supply and medical arrangements meant thousands of his men died or were incapacitated by disease.
- He stayed in Moscow for over a month before recognising the need to retreat.
- Poor planning meant that his men were not equipped for the Russian winter.

When the Grande Armée reached Germany again it was reduced to approximately 120,000 men. Napoleon left it to return swiftly to France, to restore his position there. He later blamed his defeat on the Russian winter, but historians point to the high casualties his army suffered even before the worst winter weather began.

### The War of the Sixth Coalition, 1813–14

Following the Russian disaster, the Sixth Coalition against Napoleon formed. This comprised Britain and Russia and his recent reluctant allies, initially Prussia and then also Austria. What set this coalition apart from its predecessors were five factors.

1 It had a common aim, the liberation of Germany.
2 It included all four major European powers.
3 Its members had reformed their armies and tactics.
4 France was in decline.
5 The coalition partners adopted and followed a unified military strategy.

The fighting in 1813 ended with the Battle of Leipzig, or the Battle of the Nations. Napoleon was outnumbered, defeated and forced out of Germany. The four major powers agreed the Treaty of Chaumont, March 1814. Its crucial outcome was the agreement not to make a separate peace, but to continue fighting until Napoleon was defeated.

**Identify the significance of provenance**

Study the source below.

(a) Who wrote it? What type of source is it? When and where was it written? Crucially, what was the speaker's purpose?

(b) What does this suggest about its value as a source of evidence?

## SOURCE A

Extracts from the memoires of Jakob Walter, a German conscript in Napoleon's Grande Armée. He wrote his account many years later, back in his home city of Württemberg, and intended it to be read by his family.

When we came nearer the Berezina River, there was a place where Napoleon had ordered his pack horses to be unharnessed and where he ate. He watched his army pass by in the most wretched condition. What he may have felt in his heart is impossible to surmise. His outward appearance seemed indifferent and unconcerned over the wretchedness of his soldiers; only ambition and lost honour may have made themselves felt in his heart; and, although the French and Allies shouted into his ears many oaths and curses about his own guilty person, he was still able to listen to them unmoved. After his Guard had already disbanded and he was almost abandoned, he collected a voluntary corps at Dubrovna which was enrolled with many promises and received the name of 'Holy Squadron'. After a short time, however, this existed in name only, for the enemy reduced even them to nothing.

## RAG – rate the timeline

Below are a sample exam question and a timeline. Read the question, study the timeline and, using three coloured pens, put a red, amber or green star next to the events to show:

- red: events and policies that have no relevance to the question
- amber: events and policies that have some significance to the question
- green: events and policies that are directly relevant to the question.

'Napoleon's military successes in the decade 1804–14 were due to the failings of his enemies.' Assess the validity of this view.

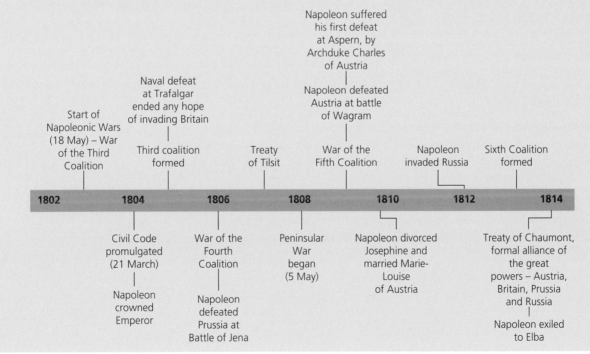

# The collapse of the Empire, part 1

Back in France Napoleon struggled to gather and equip a new army. This was difficult as France was war weary after 20 years of conscription. Finances were strained and people wanted peace. Napoleon resisted offers of negotiation and went on to win a number of small victories, but was unable to stop the numerically superior advancing armies of the Sixth Coalition. Meanwhile, he lost the political support of the Senate. By the end of March 1814 Paris had been occupied, Napoleon had abdicated and the Bourbon monarchy restored.

## The first Peace of Paris

By this treaty, negotiated by Napoleon's former foreign minister **Charles Talleyrand**, France was to lose all its territorial gains since 1792. Napoleon was exiled to the island of Elba with a pension. Meanwhile, the four major powers, once united in war, began to fall out. Britain and Austria went so far as to make a secret alliance against Prussia and Russia.

## The 100 days

In these circumstances, Napoleon thought he had an opportunity to regain power. With 700 men, he escaped from Elba on 25 February 1815. When he landed in France on 1 March, the soldiers sent to arrest him instead acclaimed him Emperor – and, as he advanced on Paris, he gained further support, while the unpopular Bourbon Louis XVIII escaped to Belgium.

Napoleon next gathered a new army with the objective of destroying the British and Prussians in Belgium before the Austrian and Russian armies could arrive. He failed and was defeated at Waterloo (18 June 1815) in what many historians see as one of the most decisive battles in European history. Napoleon's army outnumbered the British army but was unable to defeat it before the Prussians, under Blucher, arrived to win the day.

## Napoleon's abdication and second Treaty of Paris

While Napoleon wanted to continue the war, he lacked the political and popular support to do so. For a second time he had to abdicate, on 22 June 1815, and this time the British took him into a more secure exile on the isolated island of St Helena. Meanwhile, France lost more territory by the second Treaty of Paris, 20 November 1815.

## The treatment of France by the Vienna settlement

In the final settlement negotiated on behalf of France by Talleyrand at Vienna on 9 June 1815, which was now confirmed, the fate of the rest of Napoleon's Empire was decided. In some places the victors turned the clock back, in others they built upon the changes Napoleon had started. One key aim was to surround a weakened France with strong neighbours, to prevent any future attempts at expansion.

Belgium was united with Holland to create a strong state to the north, while in the south Spain was returned to its Bourbon rulers. Switzerland's independence was guaranteed. To the south-east a strengthened kingdom of Sardinia–Piedmont was created and to the north-west the German Confederation was created.

Elsewhere, Italian states were returned to Austrian influence or to their former rulers, such as the Pope in the Papal States and the Bourbons in Naples. Prussia gained control of a number of German states and Russia took most of Poland. The Empire was no more.

## Mind map

Read the question and complete the mind map with a sentence of explanation. Then prioritise your reasons by adding numbers to each box – with 1 as the most important reason and 5 as the least important.

'The long running Peninsular War was the most important reason for the military downfall of Napoleon's Empire.' Assess the validity of this view.

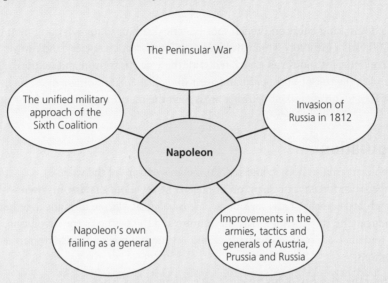

The Peninsular War

Invasion of Russia in 1812

Napoleon

The unified military approach of the Sixth Coalition

Improvements in the armies, tactics and generals of Austria, Prussia and Russia

Napoleon's own failing as a general

## Judge for yourself

**a**

Read the source, the question and the part answer provided. Highlight the sections that refer to content (and incorporate knowledge), provenance, tone and emphasis. Then use your judgement to argue why this part answer shows characteristics of a Level 5 in the mark scheme.

Assess the value of this source to a historian studying the scale of Napoleon's defeat in 1814.

This source is very valuable to the historian because it is an official, diplomatic document. It tells us exactly what was agreed between Napoleon and the victorious allies and we can reply on this being correct. It shows that they only regard Napoleon as dangerous. The rest of his family can live wherever they like. Two things are surprising. The first is the tone of the treaty. Napoleon's title as Emperor is repeatedly used and he is to be allowed to continue to use it even though the Bourbon kings are to be restored to the French throne. There is no attempt to label Napoleon as an imposter or worse. This suggests perhaps that the Tsar, who was very important in the negotiations, was not interested in humiliating his old enemy.

### SOURCE A

Extracts from the Treaty of Paris, 1814, agreed between the Emperor Napoleon and the allies.

Article 1. His Majesty the Emperor Napoleon renounces for himself, his successors and descendants, as well as for all the members of his family, all right of sovereignty and dominion, both to the French Empire and the Kingdom of Italy as well as to every other country.

Article 2. Their Majesties the Emperor Napoleon and the Empress Marie-Louise shall retain their titles and ranks, to be enjoyed during their lives. The mother, brothers, sisters, nephews and nieces of the emperor shall also retain, wherever they may reside, the title of princes of his family.

Article 3. The island of Elba, which the Emperor Napoleon has chosen as his place of his residence, shall form during his life a separate principality, which he shall possess in full sovereignty and ownership.

REVISED

## The condition of France in 1815

The Bourbon monarchy was restored but some of the key gains of the revolution remained. Feudalism no longer existed, France had a written constitution and the Civil Code ensured equality before the law for all Frenchmen. Moreover, the Concordat ensured that those who had bought land could keep it.

The years of war had a devastating effect on French society. The death of so many young men in the armies, over 900,000, was a great loss which also had a wider impact on society and future population growth. Economically, industries associated with the war effort, iron and textiles, developed as did trade with the rest of Europe. Inland areas on continental trading routes, such as Alsace on the River Rhine, prospered while other areas such the maritime ports suffered from the British blockade.

## Napoleon's reputation

The reputation of Napoleon remains hotly contested. As a man so aware of the value of propaganda while Emperor, in forced retirement on St Helena he set about shaping his own reputation, working with his secretary. Las Case's book, *Memorial de St Helena*, brought together the elements of the enduring myth – the victories, the Empire and the saving of the revolution. For others, Napoleon remained a Corsican opportunist and usurper who used France to pursue his own personal ambitions.

There is no doubt that for the majority of his time in power, France was at war and the human cost of those wars is not disputed. Some historians describe the many battlefields as hecatombs – places of great public sacrifice. The total death toll of the Napoleonic Wars was 5 million lives. But was Napoleon solely responsible? It is possible to argue that the wars were caused by four factors:

1 France's search for security and power.
2 The emergence of Russia as a European power.
3 The rivalry between Austria and Prussia.
4 The rivalry between Britain and France.

## Napoleon's legacy

There was undoubtedly a correlation between how long a territory had been part of Napoleon's Empire and how enduring his legacy was. The Napoleonic Code guaranteed civil equality wherever it was introduced and produced a legal system that was fair, cheap and not corrupt. The Concordat offered toleration to religious minorities while the gendarmerie provided law and order. These benefits can be seen as potentially balancing the human costs of the wars.

Napoleon was not a supporter of nationalism, although he utilised it where it suited his purpose, as in the case of Poland and Italy which provided so many troops for his army. By the end of the wars, however, the map of Europe was changed forever, with many of the smaller states swept away.

Napoleon also had an impact in the wider world. The Peninsular War took Spain's attention from its colonial empire. This accelerated the process of the wars of liberation in Latin American countries, while his Egyptian campaign contributed to the decline in Ottoman Empire power in the Balkans and the emergence of new states there.

**Identify the tone and emphasis of a source**

Study the source below. Don't focus on the content – instead, focus on the:
- language
- sentence structure
- emphasis of the source
- overall tone.

What does the tone and emphasis of the source suggest about its value in terms of the:
- reliability of the evidence
- utility of the evidence for studying attitudes towards Napoleon?

## SOURCE A

Extract from the memoires of the royalist Francois-René de Chateaubriand, written in 1839.

It is fashionable today to magnify Bonaparte's victories: those who suffered by them disappeared; we no longer hear the curses of the victims and their cries of pain and distress; we no longer see France exhausted with only women to till her soil ... we no longer see the conscription notices pasted up at street corners and the passers-by gathering in a crowd in front of those huge lists of dead, looking in consternation for the names of their children, their brothers, their friends, their neighbours.

**Delete as applicable** **a**

Below are a sample exam question and a paragraph written in answer to this question. Read the paragraph and decide which of the possible options (in bold) is more appropriate. Delete the less appropriate option and complete the paragraph by justifying your selection.

How important was Napoleon's legacy for Europe?

Napoleon's legacy was of **great/limited** importance for Europe. For example, the gendarmerie not only brought law and order to the territories of his Grand Empire but continued to exist even after it had been swept away by the victorious allies. So in Piedmont in Italy they were renamed the Carabinieri and remain the basis of the police force that operates to this day. The Code Napoleon had an equally important impact on people and when Prussia annexed the Rhineland in 1815 the German population insisted that the Code remain in force. These two examples go to show Napoleon's legacy was of **great/limited** importance for Europe.

On the other hand,

_____

_____

# Exam focus

Below is a sample Level 5 answer to an A-level essay question. Read the answer and the comments around it.

'The agreement of the members of the Sixth Coalition to work together was the decisive factor in the military defeat of Napoleon's Grand Empire in 1814.' Assess the validity of this view.

The agreement of Britain, Austria, Prussia and Russia to co-ordinate their military actions was a factor in Napoleon's defeat. To decide whether it was the decisive factor needs to be considered in the light of other factors. These were the lessons they had learned from their earlier failures, the crucial mistakes that Napoleon made in invading Spain in 1808 and Russia in 1812 and the weaknesses in his position in France and in his Grand Empire.

> The introduction is strong. It focuses clearly on the question, of which it shows an excellent understanding.

The Sixth Coalition against Napoleon was formed in 1816. It consisted of Britain, Austria, Prussia and Russia and it had a number of key advantages over earlier coalitions. First, its members had a common aim, to free Germany from French control. Second, all four major powers were a part of it. Third, they agreed to follow a unified military strategy. Fourth, all had improved their armies with better artillery, more flexible troop formations and new generals and tactics. Like France in the revolution, they had more effectively mobilised for war. Crucially, in March 1814 they agreed the Treaty of Chaumont. By its terms they agreed not to make a separate peace with Napoleon but to stay at war until he had been defeated.

> A short but nevertheless impressive paragraph which is very much geared to the question. The last sentence is particularly perceptive.

In the previous wars against Napoleon, the coalitions had tended to fail to act together. For example, in the war of the Fourth Coalition, Napoleon was able to defeat the Prussian army and effectively knock it out of the war before moving on to attack and defeat Russia separately, while Austria looked on from the sidelines. Or, to take the example of the War of the Third Coalition, while the Russians and Austrians fought together at Austerlitz, after the defeat Austria made a separate peace, while the Russians retreated into Russia. The second problem in those wars was that their military tactics were static and old-fashioned. In 1805 Napoleon was able to swiftly march his armies from the English Channel across Europe to catch and defeat the Austrians at Ulm in October, then move on to win the crushing victory at Austerlitz, the Battle of the Three Emperors, over the Austrians and Russians combined. That victory, considered one of his greatest, was won by his clever tactics. He deliberately weakened one flank of his army and, having enticed the enemy in, broke through their weakened centre to win a crushing victory. French casualties were 8,000. Austrian and Russian casualties were 16,000 plus 20,000 captured. The victory was also down to the superior morale and training of his army. Following those two wars, all three countries worked to improve their armies with better artillery, new tactics and new generals. This was an important factor in Napoleon's eventual defeat.

> In moving smoothly through time, this paragraph demonstrates both a command of the chronology but also a developing argument.

> This paragraph begins well, linking a key point back to the focus of the question, before losing its way a little in narrating events.

Evidence of the progress the other major powers had made was provided by events in Austrian campaign of 1809. Just as in 1805 Napoleon moved his army swiftly across Europe, this time from Spain, but when he fought the Austrians under their new general, Archduke Charles, at Aspern, he was beaten for the first time. While Napoleon went on to win his last great victory at Wagram and forced the Austrians to agree a humiliating peace treaty, where they lost much territory, this campaign showed that he could be beaten. His victories had relied upon swift movement and forcing decisive battles, but if his opponent did not let him have these, he would be in trouble. At the same time armies were getting bigger and this also made quick victories more difficult to achieve.

It was probably the great rivalry with Britain which led Napoleon into arguably his two greatest mistakes. These were the invasion of Spain in 1808 and the invasion of Russia in

> A strong paragraph in terms of well selected supporting information, although the explicit link back to the question is missing.

1812, both part of his attempt to enforce his Continental System, which was his attempt to beat the British. The Peninsular War was a massive drain on his military power – he called it the 'Spanish ulcer'. Historians suggest he lost as many men there as he did in the Russian disaster. In 1812 the Russians refused to give Napoleon the quick victory he wanted. His army only had supplies for six weeks and summer uniforms when they entered Russia in June 1812, but the Russians retreated, destroying all supplies as they did, so that Napoleon's advancing armies struggled to live off the land. When they eventually stopped to fight at Borodino they did so in the knowledge that back in 1807, at Eylau, they had been able to withstand his attacks. At the end of the day, the French won but lost 30,000 men, while the Russians lost 50,000 but were still able to retreat and refused to negotiate. In the end, Napoleon was forced to retreat and lost thousands, a disaster from which he never really recovered.

In the War of the Sixth Coalition the Battle of Leipzig, or the Battle of the Nations, was the decisive event. Napoleon was outnumbered by the Austrians, Prussians, Russians and Swedes and defeated and forced out of Germany. Military historians suggest that his style of leadership, of controlling every detail, could not work with such large forces but here, as he said, God was on the side of the big battalions. Militarily, Napoleon never recovered – his allies fell away from him as the coalition armies invaded France, including within his own regime, and he was forced to abdicate. So, in conclusion, it can be argued that he decision of the major powers to work together was the most decisive factor, although others played a part. This is reinforced by the events that followed. When the big four fell out at the Congress of Vienna, Napoleon was able to take advantage to try once again to revive his empire, a revival that ended at Waterloo.

> The conclusion weighs the relative significance of the evidence and reaches a conclusion which reflects the balance of the essay and makes a neat link to the 100 Days. The essay concludes as it began. It shows sustained analysis and a comprehensive grasp of the topic.

Level 5 answers are thorough and detailed. They clearly engage with the question and offer a balanced and carefully reasoned argument, which is sustained throughout the essay. This essay meets all the criteria for a Level 5 answer.

**Consolidation**

This is a long and detailed essay. Without losing the overall argument of the essay, experiment with reducing its length by 100 words. This is a particularly useful exercise for trying to produce an essay which gets to the heart of the question without being overlong.

# Glossary

**Absolute monarch**  Monarch who has no legal limits to their power over their subjects.

**Absenteeism**  Higher clergy like bishops not living in their dioceses, as they were pursuing a political career at court.

**Anglo-American War 1812**  War between Britain and the USA that lasted until 1815. It was prompted by British trade restrictions as part of the naval blockade of France, the seizure of hundreds of US sailors for the Royal Navy and tensions in North America.

**Assignats**  Bonds backed up by the sale of Church land, that circulated as a form of paper money.

**Austrian Committee**  Politicians gathered around Marie Antoinette who, according to popular conspiracy suspicions, were in treasonous secret contact with Austria.

**Battle of Trafalgar (1805)**  Key British naval victory in which Admiral Nelson destroyed the combined French and Spanish fleets thus securing control of the seas.

**Billeted**  When soldiers are lodged in peoples' houses, which was greatly resented in France.

**Bourgeoisie**  Originally meaning 'the citizens of a town', by 1789 the term described the middle classes. These included merchants, industrialists, business people, financiers, landowners, doctors, lawyers and civil servants.

**Brigands**  Gangs of robbers operating in area where the forces of law and order were weak.

**Cahiers de doléances**  Lists of grievances and suggestions for reform drawn up by the three orders for the meeting of the Estates-General.

**Catechisms**  Summary of Christian teaching in the form of questions and answers.

**Chouans**  Royalist rebels in western France who were usually peasants.

**Citizen's militia**  Defence force composed of bourgeois Parisians, set up to protect property. It later became the National Guard.

**Civisme**  Good citizenship, being a good citizen.

**Clemency**  Mercy.

**Clichien**  Member of the club that formed under the Directory, who tended to be moderate constitutional monarchists and opponents of the neo-Jacobins.

**Commission**  Military or naval officer posts had to be bought. Therefore all officers were nobles.

**Committee of General Security (CGS)**  Committee of National Convention deputies that kept a watch on state security and foreign agents.

**Committee of Public Safety (CPS)**  Committee of National Convention deputies that came to be a war cabinet.

**Commune**  Municipal government of Paris.

**Conscription**  Compulsory enrolment of men into the armed forces.

**Constitutional monarchy**  Political system where the powers of the monarch are limited by a constitution.

**Court factions**  Groupings of nobles at court, including the queen and the king's brothers, who pursued policies that benefited them or that they approved of.

**Curé**  Parish priest who, in the countryside, was often the only educated person in the village.

**Custom posts**  Part of the internal barriers to trade around Paris, where taxes on goods coming into the city had to be paid.

**Dauphin**  Heir to the French throne.

**Dechristianisation**  Movement to destroy the French Catholic Church and the practice of religion.

**Deflation**  General reduction in prices in an economy.

**Departments**  Divisions of France for elections and local government, introduced in 1790.

**Despot**  Monarch or ruler who exercises absolute power, especially in a cruel or oppressive way.

**'Dry guillotine'**  Term used to describe the punishment of exile to the French colony of Guiana, as so many exiles died of tropical diseases.

**Election credentials**  Verification of the legality of the election of a deputy.

**Émigrés**  Nobles who had emigrated from France since the revolution began including Louis's brothers.

**Enrages**  Insulting term, 'angry ones', used to describe militants.

**Estates-General**  Body containing representatives of all three estates of France – Church, nobility and Third Estate – called in times of national emergency. It last met in 1614.

**Farmers-General**  Syndicate of men who every six years contracted with the Crown to collect certain taxes such as the taille. With a staff of roughly 30,000 they were the largest employer in France after the king's army and navy.

**fédérés**  Provincial National Guards.

**feudalism/feudal rights**  System by which peasants held land in return for some of their labour and their produce.

**Gardes-françaises**  French royal infantry regiment.

**Généralités**   Thirty-six administrative regions into which Ancien Régime France was divided.

**Gilded Youth**   Gangs of young men in Paris, organised by Stanislas Fréron.

**Girondins**   Small group of deputies from the Gironde area and their associates. The most notable was Brissot.

**Grapeshot**   Ammunition consisting of a number of small iron balls fired together from a cannon.

**Guerrilla warfare**   Irregular warfare carried out by the people of an area against larger regular armies.

**Holy Roman Empire**   Empire composed of a number of territories in central Europe that developed during the Middle Ages and continued until its dissolution in 1806.

**Indulgents**   Faction led by Danton who campaigned for an end to the Terror in early 1794.

**Intendant**   Ancien Régime royal official in charge of a Généralité.

**Jacobins**   Name given to Dominican monks in Paris. When the Breton deputies began to hold their meetings in the Jacobin's former convent they were mockingly called Jacobins by their opponents in the National Assembly, suggesting they were some sort of monks.

**Journée**   A day of popular action and disturbance linked to great political change such as the storming of the Bastille.

**Justice of the Peace**   New official based on the English model. JPs were elected by active citizens, one per canton, to serve for two years, making judgements on cases up to the value of 50 livres.

**laissez-faire**   Government policy of non-interference in the workings of the economy.

**Legion of Honour**   Order introduced by Napoleon to reward military and civil merits.

**Lit de Justice**   Formal session of a parlement, during which the monarch could forcibly register an edict over riding the parlement's objections.

**Livres**   Basic currency of France until 7 April 1795. 1 louis = 24 livres, 1 livre = 20 sous, 1 sou = 12 deniers.

**Masonic Lodges**   Local secret societies set up to fund charities, but more importantly places where men could debate the new ideas about society and government. Between 1773 and 1779 over 20,000 men joined.

**neo-Jacobins**   New Jacobins, the left-wing group who emerged after Thermidor.

**Parlement**   High courts of appeal that combined legal and administrative functions. All edicts from the Crown had to be ratified by the parlements before they could be enforced. There were 13 in 1789.

**Partage**   An estate should be divided equally among all the male heirs.

**Physiocrats**   Economists who believed that the wealth of the nation came solely from agriculture and that all state regulations, tolls and price controls should be ended.

**Plebiscite**   Popular vote on a single issue, a feature of Napoleon's France that allowed him to appeal over the heads of the political classes directly to the people.

**Polignac clique**   The Polignac clique were members of the Polignac family and their friends were close to Marie Antoinette.

**Poor relief**   Payments of food given to the poor by the Catholic Church.

**Prefects**   Officials placed in charge of a Department in Napoleonic France.

**Princes of the Blood**   The King's seven closest male relatives, including his brothers, the Comte de Provence and the Comte d'Artois and his cousin, Louis, Duc D'Orleans.

**Ratified**   Formally approved before it could become officially valid.

**Refractory clergy**   Clergy who refused to swear an oath of loyalty to the Constitution.

**Representatives on mission**   National Convention deputies sent to the provinces, two to each, and to the armies to make sure government policy was followed. They had wide reaching powers.

**Salon**   Event hosted by an aristocratic woman to which invited a range of guests, nobles and bourgeoisie to discuss art, literature and politics.

**Sans-culottes**   Name coined in 1791 for the small property owners, shopkeepers and workers, both masters and their employees, who came out in support of the revolution.

**Scorched earth**   Military strategy of destroying everything that might be useful to an enemy.

**Séance royale**   Royal Session of the Estates-General attended by all three estates.

**Seigneur**   Lord of a manor who held seigneurial or feudal rights over the peasants.

**Seven Years' War (1756–63)**   France, in alliance with Austria, was defeated by Britain and Prussia.

**Subsistence farming**   Growing enough food to feed yourself and your family with nothing left over for sale.

**Terrorists**   Name given to Robespierre and his associates after Thermidor, putting the blame for the Terror on them.

**Tithe**   Tax paid to the Church of one-tenth of annual produce.

**Venal office**   Official job or post that could be bought, which gave its holder noble status.

**Veto**   Constitutional right to reject a proposal by a law-making body.

# Key figures

**Georges-Jacques Danton (1759–94, guillotined)**
Lawyer who emerged as an early leader of the Cordeliers, involved in the overthrow of Louis XVI. Appointed Minister of Justice of the Provisional Executive Committee, he failed to prevent the September massacres but did rally the capital for the war effort. He campaigned for an end to the Terror, to which he fell victim.

**Joseph Fouché, Duke of Otranto (1758–1820)**
National Convention deputy sent as a representative on mission to Lyons where he organised the mitraillades. Threatened by Robespierre, he helped plot Thermidor, before dropping out of politics until he became Minister of Police in 1799, a role in which he continued under Napoleon.

**Jacques-Rene Hébert (1757–94, guillotined)**
Began publishing the radical journal, *Père Duchesne*, in 1789. He was active in the Cordeliers Club, in the Paris Commune and the overthrow of Louis XVI. A radical thinker, he continually argued for more Terror as well as being part of the dechristianisation movement. Following his attacks on the Indulgents he was arrested and convicted.

**Marquis de Lafayette (1757–1834)** Liberal noble who fought in the American War of Independence. He was appointed commander of the new Parisian National Guard, but lost popularity for his support of constitutional monarchy and his part in the Champ de Mars massacre. As a revolutionary general, he tried to turn his army on Paris and, when that failed, defected to the enemy. He returned to live in France under Napoleon.

**Louis XVI (King of France 1774–92, b.1754, guillotined 1793)** Inherited the throne from his grandfather, Louis XV. While he was successful in the American War of Independence, he never resolved the financial problems of the Crown. He failed to follow a consistent course in the early stages of the revolution and the flight to Varennes lost him much popularity. Following the failure of constitutional monarchy, for which he was in part responsible, he was overthrown, imprisoned, tried and executed for treason.

**Marie Antoinette (Queen of France 1774–93, guillotined)** Austrian-born Queen of France. She damaged the prestige of the monarchy with her alleged extravagance and involvement in scandals. She opposed compromise with the revolutionaries and pursued the full restoration of Louis XVI's powers. She was viewed as head of the shadowy Austrian Committee and did pass military information to the Austrians in 1792.

**Jean-Paul Marat (1744–1793)** Radical revolutionary journalist implicated in the September massacres. His impeachment was a key factor in the fall of the Girondins. His assassination by Charlotte Corday in part triggered the Terror.

**Napoleon Bonaparte (Emperor 1804–15, b.1769)**
Son of a Corsican lawyer who trained for the army in France and rose to high command during the revolution. Under the Directory, his brilliant victories in Italy gave him the popularity to be able to seize power in the Coup of Brumaire. Therafter, he ruled France as consul and then Emperor until his forced abdication in 1815.

**Jacques Necker (1732–1804)** Genevan banker who served as finance minister 1777–81. His second spell in government was unsuccessful. He mishandled the Estates-General and was in Switzerland when the fall of the Bastille forced Louis to recall him. He was marginalised by the workings of the Constituent Assembly and emigrated in 1790.

**Maximilien Robespierre (1764–94, guillotined)**
Son of a lawyer who came to national prominence having been elected to the Estates-General in 1789. He was very influential in the Jacobin Club, instrumental in the overthrow and execution of the king and acted as spokesman for the Committee of Public Safety on which he served 1793–94.

**Jean-Jacques Rousseau (1712–88)** One of the leading philosophes who wrote, among other works, *The Social Contract*. He argued that a despotic monarch could be overthrown by their subjects and that sovereignty resided in the people rather than in the person of the king. His ideas were very influential on many revolutionaries, including Robespierre and Madam Roland.

**Abbe Sieyès (1748–1836)** Emmanuel-Joseph Sieyès was born into a bourgeois family, trained for the Church and ordained in 1773. Influenced by Rousseau, he supported reform. He wrote the pamphlet, *What is the Third Estate?*, served as a deputy to the Estates-General, helped draw up the Tennis Court Oath and the Rights of Man. Thereafter, his influence waned. A supporter of constitutional monarchy, he voted for the death of the king but kept a low profile during the Terror. After Robespierre's fall he regained influence and plotted the coup of Brumaire. Out-manoeuvred by Napoleon, he retired from public life.

**Charles Talleyrand (1754–1838)** He was a bishop in 1789, when he entered the Estates-General as a deputy, but renounced it after the Civil Constitution of the clergy. He was exiled after the overthrow of the monarchy but returned to serve as Foreign Minister under the Directory, then Napoleon and then the restored Bourbons.

# Timeline

| 1774 | Accession of Louis XIV |
| 1776 | Turgot appointed |
| 1778 | France entered the American War of Independence against Britain |
| 1781 | Necker resigned |
| 1783 | Peace of Paris |
| | Calonne appointed finance minister |
| 1787 | Meeting of the Assembly of Notables |
| 1788 | Estates-General called for 1789 |
| | Payments from the Treasury suspended |
| | Second Assembly of Notables |
| | Royal decree to double the number of third estate deputies |
| 1789 | Sieyès published *What is the Third Estate?* |
| | Opening of the Estates-General at Versailles |
| | National Assembly claimed national sovereignty |
| | Tennis Court Oath |
| | Fall of the Bastille |
| | The Great Fear in the countryside |
| | October Days |
| 1790 | Feudalism abolished |
| | Civil Constitution of the Clergy |
| 1791 | Flight to Varennes |
| | Champ de Mars massacre |
| | Pillnitz Declaration |
| 1792 | War declared on Austria |
| | Publication of the Brunswick Manifesto |
| | Overthrow of the monarchy |
| 1793 | Trial and execution of Louis XVI |
| | Revolutionary Tribunal created |
| | Revolt in the Vendée began |
| | Committee of Public Safety created |
| | Federalist revolts – Bordeaux, Caen and Lyons |
| | Levée en masse decree issued |
| | Girondins executed |
| 1794 | Hébertists and Dantonists executed |
| | The Law of Prairial |
| | Thermidor – fall of Robespierre |
| | End of the Terror |
| 1795 | White Terror in southern France |
| | Vendémiaire uprising in Paris |
| | Directory inaugurated |
| 1796 | Napoleon appointed Commander in Italy |
| 1797 | Treaty of Campo Formio with Austria |
| 1798 | Napoleon's Egyptian campaign |
| 1799 | War of the Second Coalition |
| | Brumaire coup – Napoleon took power |

| 1800 | Bank of France founded |
| | Napoleon won Battle of Marengo |
| | Failed assassination attempt on Napoleon |
| 1801 | Concordat with the Pope |
| 1802 | Peace of Amiens – end of Revolutionary Wars |
| | Tribunate purged for opposing the Civil Code |
| | Napoleon made First Consul for Life |
| 1803 | Britain declared war on France, start of Napoleonic Wars, War of the Third Coalition |
| 1804 | Execution of the Duc d'Enghien |
| | Civil Code promulgated |
| | Napoleon crowned Emperor (December) |
| 1805 | Third coalition formed |
| | Naval defeat at Trafalgar |
| | Napoleon won the Battle of Austerlitz |
| 1806 | Creation of the Confederation of the Rhine |
| | War of Fourth Coalition |
| | Napoleon defeated Prussians at battle of Jena |
| 1807 | Napoleon defeated Russians at the Battles of Eylau and Friedland |
| | Treaty of Tilsit |
| | Creation of the Kingdom of Westphalia and the Duchy of Poland |
| | Napoleonic Code introduced to Europe |
| 1808 | Peninsular War began |
| | Legislature abolished |
| 1809 | War of the Fifth Coalition |
| | Napoleon suffered his first defeat at Aspern |
| | Napoleon defeated Austrians at the Battle of Wagram |
| 1810 | Napoleon divorced Josephine and married Marie-Louise of Austria |
| 1812 | Britain and the USA at war |
| | Napoleon invaded Russia |
| 1813 | Sixth Coalition formed |
| | Napoleon defeated at Battle of Leipzig |
| 1814 | Treaty of Chaumont, formal alliance of the great powers – Austria, Britain, Prussia and Russia |
| | Paris surrendered, Talleyrand head of provisional government |
| | First Bourbon Restoration |
| | First Treaty of Paris |
| | Napoleon exiled to Elba |
| | Congress of Vienna opened |
| 1815 | The 100 Days |
| | Battle of Waterloo |
| | Napoleon's abdication |
| | Second Bourbon Restoration |

# Answers

## Page 11, Complete the paragraph

Overall the three groups, while all nobles, were very different. The court nobility's monopoly of power was resented by the other two groups. The noblesse de robe were looked down upon by the others and while some nobles welcomed the new Enlightenment ideas the majority did not so while they appeared to be a single group there were in fact deep divisions between them.

## Page 13, Moving from assertion to argument

The Enlightenment was an important factor in the coming of the French Revolution because its scientific approach directly challenged ideas held by the Church and other institutions and caused great controversy. Its ideas on social and political issues challenged the very basis of the Ancien Régime.

Among the Philosophes Rousseau believed that the people could overthrow a despotic ruler. This idea was dangerous because to some Louis XVI was an absolute and despotic ruler with such powers as the ability to imprison without trial.

People heard and read Enlightenment arguments in a variety of places such as aristocratic salons, the theatre, bookshops, Masonic Lodges and they read about them in newspapers, books and the Encyclopaedia.

This was important because the ideas reached a wide audience through so many different routes and had a significant influence upon peoples' thinking.

In many ways the Enlightenment was a **very important** factor to the coming of the Revolution.

## Page 15, Support or challenge?

The following statements support:
- The war cost 1.3 billion livres (the war was incredibly expensive as annual government income in 1775 was just over 411 million livres)
- Louis inherited a massive debt from his predecessors (Louis simply could not afford to go to war as the burden of his existing debts was already so high)

The following statements challenge:
- Louis XVI's ministers failed to make financial reforms (it was really this failure that led to the failure of royal finances, although you can argue the war decision speeded the process up)

- The French tax system was inefficient (longer term the failures of the system were responsible for the problem rather than any short term decision making)
- The Parlement of Paris refused to agree to new taxes (because even at that later stage a solution to royal finances might have been found, although you could counter this argument by arguing that the royal debt had grown so big, over 40 per cent of government income spent on debt interest payments)

## Page 15, Judgements on the value of a source

Answer 3 is the better response because it gives a balanced assessment of the value of the source and explicitly comments upon key aspects of provenance including purpose and utility.

## Page 25, Judgements on the value of a source

Answer 2 is the better response because it evaluates the content, gives a balanced assessment of the value of the source and explicitly comments upon the key aspect of provenance including typicality and utility.

## Page 29, Spectrum of importance

Most important:
- 4 The ideas of leading revolutionaries – were heavily influenced by Enlightenment ideas
- 5 The aristocratic revolt – the link can be made to Montesquieu's view that it was the role of the aristocracy to limit royal power
- 1 The number of Masonic lodges, theatres and bookshops in towns and cities – ensured many people were exposed to Enlightenment ideas
- 3 The abolition of feudalism – can be linked to Enlightenment ideas on freedom and equality

Least important:
- 6 The failure of Louis XVI's financial reforms – this was more the result of entrenched positions and a lack of consistent policy
- 2 The October Days – a response of ordinary people to hard times

## Page 31, Judge for yourself

The answer shows some understanding of the provenance and typicality of the two sources and shows awareness of the context, for example the Clerical Oath and refractory priests. It therefore exhibits characteristics of a Level 4 answer.

## Page 37, Support or challenge?

The following statements support:

- During the September Massacres 1,500 prisoners were murdered (the most bloody of a number of episodes of revolutionary violence)
- The Insurrectionist Committee organised the armed overthrow of the monarchy on 10 August 1792 (direct use of violence, although some argue that the Swiss Guards were responsible for the outbreak of fighting on the day)

The following statements challenge:

- Louis moved troops into the Paris and Versailles area in 1789 (it can be argued that the king, with the power of the army behind him, threatened the use of force against the National Assembly Deputies)
- The garrison of the Bastille fired first on 14 July 1789 (while accounts differ, the people only wanted the munitions, no lives were lost when munitions were taken earlier from Les Invalides)
- Revolutionaries were eager to declare war on Austria in 1792 (this war was promoted by both revolutionaries and the monarchy if for different motives
- The Brunswick Manifesto (1792) threatened vengeance on Paris (written by émigrés and issued by the General of an invading army, this again was violence being offered by the counter-revolutionary forces)

## Page 45, Delete as applicable

The Girondins in the National Convention were successful to a **limited** extent. For example, they persuaded the deputies to hold a trial. The Montagnards viewed him as guilty already and believed a trial was unnecessary. The Girondins were also successful in getting a conviction. However, they wanted to keep Louis as a bargaining chip and didn't want the sentence to be death. In this respect they were outmanoeuvred by the Montagnards who ensured that the deputies had to cast their vote publicly on what sentence to give, imprisonment or death. In this way, the Girondins in the National Assembly were **not** successful because *Louis went to the guillotine in 1793. Moreover from then on the Girondins were effectively in conflict with the Montagnards, a political struggle which was ended when the Montagnards, using the support of the sans-culottes, overthrew the Girondins and sent them in their turn to the guillotine.*

## Page 49, Spot the mistake

This paragraph does not get beyond Level 2 because it has failed to grasp the demands of the question which asks

'how dangerous was the Federalist revolt'. Instead, this answer explains where and why the revolt occurred.

## Page 49, Turning assertion into argument

The first answer reaches a higher level on the mark scheme. This is because it builds an argument for Robespierre's importance by explaining the significance of each action or event. The second answer merely makes a number of reasonable assertions about Robespierre. It therefore exhibits the characteristics of a Level 2 answer.

## Page 53, Comparing two alternative answers

The first answer is the better answer. It makes a judgement on which is the better source, A, and begins to support that by reference to the content of both, limited discussion of their provenance and some reference t the tone of Source B. This answer exhibits some of the characteristics of a Level 2 answer.

The second answer does little more than describe source content and exhibits the characteristics of a Level 1 answer.

## Page 63, Judgements on the value of a source

Answer 2 is the better response because it considers the provenance of the source more fully to comment on its value and its limitations for the issue identified in the question.

## Page 79, Judgements on the value of a source

Answer 2 is the better response because it considers the provenance of the source more fully, drawing upon understanding of the historical context to comment on its value and its limitations for the issue identified in the question.

## Page 83, Develop the detail

Between 1804 and 1814 Napoleon and his government took a number of steps to ensure the financial stability of his regime. New ministries **of the Treasury and Finance** and offices **such as the Audit Office** were set up and new ministers were appointed. **In the Ministry of Finance, Martin Gaudin was appointed and served right up to 1814. He was responsible for the improved collection of taxation and revenues.** The Bank of France was set up in 1800 and Napoleon supported and controlled this. The centralisation of government allowed Napoleon to make a number of changes to the tax system, both direct and indirect taxes, with the result that more tax income was raised. **Land registers showing ownership were drawn up and** the tax registers showing who should pay were improved. **These steps made its collection fair and efficient. New indirect taxes were levied on wine, playing cards and, most controversially in 1806, salt. Income from these increased by over 400 per cent between 1806 and 1812.** He also brought in a new currency, **the franc**, based upon metal rather than paper. Altogether these measures led to more stable government finances.

## Page 93, Complete the paragraph

Overall, this policy was a success, as Napoleon kept control of his Grand Empire for over five years. His problems in the Iberian Peninsula were due to a range of factors, not just the rule of his brother Joseph, and it was noticeable that a number of non-family members who he promoted were not loyal to him, notably Marshal Bernadotte in Sweden, but also men like his ministers of police, Fouché, and of foreign affairs, Talleyrand.

## Page 93, Moving from assertion to argument

Napoleon's Grand Empire was large because ... by 1811 it consisted of an expanded France up to its natural frontiers, a number of annexed territories, for example, Piedmont, Tuscany and satellite states, for example, Kingdoms of Italy, Holland, Westphalia ... and this meant that ... it was physically difficult to control with not just distances but differing nationalities and political systems to contend with.

Napoleon was able to make use of family members and trusted Generals to run parts of his Empire and this was ... a successful strategy. In only three regions was there armed rebellion – Calabria in Naples, the Tyrol in Austria, and Spain.

When Napoleon invaded Russia in 1812 he was able to do so with an army of 600,000 men. This was because ... not only could he draw finance and manpower from France itself and its annexed territories, but also from the satellite states. They provided roughly half Napoleon's military expenditure in the decade 1804 to 1814.

## Page 101, Judge for yourself

The answer demonstrates good understanding of the source in relation to its content and provenance, linking these with strong awareness of the historical context. For example, the crucial point that Napoleon is treated quite leniently is linked to the importance of the Tsar, who admired him, in the negotiations. That it is a formal written document is self-evident, but its respectful tone is also noted.

## Page 103, Delete as applicable

Napoleon's legacy was of **great** importance for Europe. For example, the gendarmerie not only brought law and order to the territories of his Grand Empire but continued to exist even after it had been swept away by the victorious allies. So in Piedmont in Italy they were renamed the Carabinieri and remain the basis of the police force that operates to this day. The Code Napoleon had an equally important impact on people and when Prussia annexed the Rhineland in 1815 the German population insisted that the Code remain in force. These two examples go to show Napoleon's legacy was of **great** importance for Europe.

On the other hand, *his own claims of supporting nationalism are less convincing. He was prepared to stoke the fires of patriotism in Poland and Italy but his motives were not so much to create nation states but rather to ensure short term military support. He changed the map of Europe certainly but cannot be credited with the creation of new nation states.*